Praise for
Are You a Stock or a Bond?

"Milevsky guides us through the perilous financial wilderness in pursuit of the promised land of a secure retirement. Milevsky has the rare gift to illuminate abstract financial and mathematical concepts in everyday language and experiences. A must-read in this age of the growing burden on individuals to shoulder greater responsibility for their financial security in retirement."

> —Steven Siegel, Research Actuary,
> Society of Actuaries

"The author provides a holistic approach to lifetime financial planning and discusses cutting-edge ideas about how you should manage your asset allocation, demand for insurance, and many other financial decisions. In this book, Milevsky demonstrates his unique ability to explain key financial concepts using down-to-earth language."

> —Dr. William Reichenstein, CFA,
> Baylor University

"Milevsky brings much recent research to bear in trying to help people use concepts of modern financial economics in integrated personal financial planning. A key element he brings to the forefront here is understanding the role individual labor income, lifestyle, and longevity play in modern dynamic portfolio theory."

> —Sid Browne, Ph.D.,
> Brevan Howard Asset Management and Columbia Business School

"This book is a must-read for anyone who desires life-long financial security. Those who read it will have a much deeper understanding of how concepts such as 'human capital' and 'risk management' are not arcane academic terms, but rather concepts that provide an extraordinarily useful road map for creating lasting financial security."

> —Jeffrey R. Brown, Professor of Finance,
> University of Illinois at Urbana-Champaign

ARE YOU A
STOCK
OR A
BOND?

ARE YOU A
STOCK
OR A
BOND?

CREATE YOUR OWN PENSION PLAN
FOR A SECURE FINANCIAL FUTURE

MOSHE A. MILEVSKY

Vice President, Publisher: Tim Moore
Associate Publisher and Director of Marketing: Amy Neidlinger
Executive Editor: Jim Boyd
Editorial Assistant: Myesha Graham
Development Editor: Russ Hall
Digital Marketing Manager: Julie Phifer
Publicity Manager: Laura Czaja
Assistant Marketing Manager: Megan Colvin
Cover Designer: Sandra Schroeder
Operations Manager: Gina Kanouse
Managing Editor: Kristy Hart
Project Editor: Anne Goebel
Copy Editor: Paula Lowell
Proofreader: San Dee Phillips
Indexer: WordWise Publishing Services, LLC
Senior Compositor: Gloria Schurick
Manufacturing Buyer: Dan Uhrig

© 2009 by Pearson Education, Inc.
Publishing as FT Press
Upper Saddle River, New Jersey 07458

FT Press offers excellent discounts on this book when ordered in quantity for bulk purchases or special sales. For more information, please contact U.S. Corporate and Government Sales, 1-800-382-3419, corpsales@pearsontechgroup.com. For sales outside the U.S., please contact International Sales at international@pearson.com.

Company and product names mentioned herein are the trademarks or registered trademarks of their respective owners.

Printed in the United States of America
Second Printing August 2008
ISBN-10: 0-13-712737-5
ISBN-13: 978-0-13-712737-5

Pearson Education LTD.
Pearson Education Australia PTY, Limited.
Pearson Education Singapore, Pte. Ltd.
Pearson Education North Asia, Ltd.
Pearson Education Canada, Ltd.
Pearson Educatión de Mexico, S.A. de C.V.
Pearson Education—Japan
Pearson Education Malaysia, Pte. Ltd.

Library of Congress Cataloging-in-Publication Data

Milevsky, Moshe Arye, 1967-
Are you a stock or a bond? : create your own pension plan for a secure financial future / Moshe A. Milevsky.
    p. cm.
Includes bibliographical references.
ISBN 0-13-712737-5 (hbk. : alk. paper) 1. Finance, Personal. 2. Investments. I. Title.
HG179.M4577 2009
332.024—dc22
                2008005434

This book is dedicated to my mother, Chaya Milevsky-Mannes, whose energy has inspired me for the last 40 years.

Contents

Acknowledgments

This book would have been impossible to research and write without the help of some key people at The IFID Centre and York University. I would like to start by acknowledging Anna Abaimova (IFID Centre), Alexa Brand (IFID Centre), Brandon Walker (IFID Centre), and Vlad Kyrychenko (IFID Centre), who helped with many aspects of the manuscript preparation and editing. I would also like to thank my colleagues, mentors, and friends—Thomas Salisbury (IFID Centre/York University), Huaxiong Huang (IFID Centre/York University), Chris Robinson (Atkinson/York University), Virginia Young (University of Michigan), David Promislow (IFID Centre/York University), Peng Chen (Ibbotson / Morningstar), Sid Browne (Columbia University/Goldman Sachs), Steven Posner (Morgan Stanley), and Lowell Aronoff (CANNEX Financial)—with whom I have had numerous discussions and productive collaborations over the years. I would also like to thank Gil Weinreich (Research Magazine), Mike Orszag (Watson Wyatt), and Francois Gadenne (RIIA) for helping extend the reach and scope of my research work. Also, Jim Boyd, Paula Lowell, Anne Goebel (all three at Pearson Education), and Marc Reede (Nationwide Speakers) deserve special acknowledgment. Finally, no thank-you is complete without mentioning Edna Diena-Milevsky (my wife), who carefully reviewed the manuscript to make sure I was speaking English at all times.

About the Author

Moshe Milevsky lectures at the Schulich School of Business, York University, Toronto, where he became a professor and earned his Ph.D. at the age of 27 and received academic tenure at the age of 33. He is also the executive director of the nonprofit IFID Centre (www.ifid.ca) which he launched in the summer of 2000. He has published five books and more than 50 peer-reviewed articles on the topic of pensions, insurance, investments, derivative pricing, and retirement income planning. He was the founding co-editor in 2002 of the *Journal of Pension Economics and Finance* and the author of the 2006 book *The Calculus of Retirement Income*, both published by Cambridge University Press. He has delivered seminars at the London School of Economics, the Wharton Business School, and the University of Michigan, as well as universities in Europe and South America. Dr. Milevsky was honored as a Fields Institute Fellow in the summer of 2002 for his contributions to mathematics. He was recognized for his research on practical financial planning by the CFA Institute in 2006 when he received a Graham and Dodd scroll award for an article he cowrote and published in the *Financial Analysts Journal*. Finally, in addition to his scholarly activities, in early October 2006, he was co-awarded a U.S. patent number (7,120,601B2) for his invention, "optimal asset allocation during retirement...with life annuities."

Preface

How Much Risk Are You Really Handling?

I normally don't speak to anybody on airplanes unless it is absolutely necessary, preferring instead to mind my own business, catch up on emails, or fill in paperwork. However, when the attractive, middle-aged lady sitting next to me on the flight from Dallas to Boston asked me whether the article I was reading was interesting, I decided to break my long-standing aviation rule and take up the conversation.

Apparently, Kimberly—or Kim as she preferred to be called—was flying to a job interview at a large and well-known financial services company headquartered on the east coast. She was rather apprehensive about the interview because the advertised area was completely new to her, and she didn't have much experience or knowledge of the financial industry. Being a professor of finance myself, it was fun and easy for me to offer some tips and trends.

As we chatted, it became apparent that she had recently lost her job at a medium-sized manufacturing company around the Dallas area—a casualty of cheaper labor and products from overseas—and was instead trying her luck in a completely different field. Her extensive expertise and knowledge of a particular software program used by her previous employer was of little use outside of the narrow manufacturing sector in which she had spent the last decade of her life. So, she was basically starting from scratch.

To make matters worse for Kim, although she was employed at the Dallas-based company for more than eight years, she didn't have much savings accumulated in her employer-sponsored, tax-sheltered savings plan. The company didn't offer a traditional pension plan, which actually had been frozen years ago. Indeed, the bulk of her tax-sheltered (aka 401k) savings plan had been allocated to one mutual fund and the common stock of the company she actually worked for. Neither of these investments had done very well in the last few years, and her account value was well under the cost basis of the funds.

Basically, it was worth much less than the sum of all the money she had ever invested in the plan. The reason she had allocated so much to this one stock is because the company offered a matching deal. Every $100 of salary she deferred and contributed to the 401(k) plan would be matched by the company with $50 of company stock. Effectively, she was getting a 50% investment return on her money, from day one—and it was tax deferred. At first glance, this is a great deal, and many companies offer the same plan. Unfortunately, though, her company's stock price had fallen by more than 60% in the last 18 months, which basically wiped out the gains. In fact, the day she and more than 1,000 other employees were let go, the stock price fell a further 15%, likely because the company announced a major restructuring at the same time.

I obviously felt bad for her, although she seemed to be dealing with her financial misfortune with great poise. She was actually looking forward to starting a new job and perhaps new life working in the financial services industry in Boston. She said it reminded her of graduating from college almost 15 years ago with no savings, no relevant work experience, and a bunch of credit card debt. What a great, positive attitude.

As the flight continued and the conversation evolved, it turns out that she was recently separated from her husband, who coincidently had also been laid off from the same employer on the exact same day. Kim had originally met him at a company picnic a number of years ago, and they had much in common, including a shared employer and career prospects. But, the stress of the dual job loss and the ensuing financial strain had taken a toll on their marriage, and the two of them were in the process of selling their house, which was located a short commute from their old employer, while working out the divorce proceedings.

As if the stress of a job loss wasn't enough, unfortunately, the real estate market wasn't being kind to them either. The house was apparently now worth 20% less than what they had paid a few years ago, and they were having a very tough time getting any offers on the house. I suspected that this difficulty is likely because a number of other residents in the neighborhood, who had also been laid off recently, were also trying to sell their homes at the same time.

Kim was hoping that they would eventually be able to sell the house for at least the value of the mortgage, which, of course, is the amount they actually owed the bank. Otherwise, they might be faced with the terrible possibility of having to file for bankruptcy, or perhaps even face foreclosure. Apparently, Kim and her husband had financed the purchase of their house with an adjustable rate mortgage (ARM) whose underlying interest rate had just been reset to a higher level. The monthly payments were now double what they were two years ago.

As you might suspect by this point in the narrative, I never actually met a Kimberly on an airplane to Boston. I'm sure there are many Kimberlys out there; I just haven't met them yet. I made up her and her very gloomy life just to make a point. Many nice people who have successful jobs, lovely houses, and hefty 401(k) accounts are destined to be Kimberly. They just don't know it yet.

These individuals have placed too many of their life eggs in one basket. They have, unfortunately, allocated their careers, houses, investment portfolios, and even marriages into one economic sector. They have thus violated the most important rule of modern financial theory, and that is to *diversify your risk factors*. Many people incorrectly believe that diversification only applies and is relevant to the stocks and bonds in your investment accounts. The truth is that it should be applied to anything that has the potential to generate an income or cash flow. Diversification should be applied to all the stocks and bonds in your daily life, not just to your financial portfolio.

In today's volatile economic environment and financial markets, investors are constantly reevaluating their attitude to financial risk on virtually a daily basis. During the times and periods stock markets are in positive territory and increasing in value, the masses believe they are risk tolerant. Then, in the next week, month, or year when markets decline sharply, they decide they are risk averse and can't handle the volatility. They sell out, liquidate, and miss-time the market. Their attitude to financial risk is more fickle than the markets themselves, and risk-aversion becomes an elusive temperament without a solid foundation. It is, therefore, almost meaningless to ask people what their risk attitude is. It changes based on yesterday's market, today's mood, and even tomorrow's weather. How can one make investment decisions regarding hundreds of thousands of dollars based on the answer to a question that changes daily?

This book argues that your approach to financial risk should *not* be based on a psychological mindset based on your temper *du jour*, but instead on the composition of your entire personal balance sheet. My main message is that YOU must start approaching your financial situation in a more holistic manner. Your house, your city, your job, your marriage, and even your health is a financial asset that must coexist and be diversified with the rest of the financial assets and liabilities on your personal balance sheet. In this book, I explain why this holistic diversification is so important and how you can do it.

In the past, a financial portfolio of stocks and bonds was more of a perk than a necessity. The investment account was a retirement income supplement or perhaps a part-time hobby. Today, your stocks and bonds—very broadly defined—will become the means by which you will be able to finance and support the last 20 or 30 years of your life. You owe it to yourself to base these decisions on more than "do you feel lucky today?"

Introduction

Pensions Are Dying; Long Live Pensions

"…At present, the only way a company can manage the risk of long-lived workers is to work them so hard that they die within a few years of retirement; this is not a good way to retain staff…."

Financial Times, editorial, September 30, 2006

On Tuesday, March 7, 2006, General Motors (GM) issued a press release that was distributed to newswires and the usual business channels. In a briefly worded statement, it announced that all new employees hired by GM after January 1, 2007, would no longer be entitled to enroll or participate in the company's traditional pension plan. The plan was being closed and frozen to all entrants. Instead, new GM employees would be given the option of participating in the company's enhanced salary-deferred, tax-sheltered savings program, also known as a 401(k) plan. Employees who elected to join the 401(k) plan would have their contributions or savings matched by GM, up to a limit, as is usually the case with these ubiquitous plans. They would be given the ability to manage and diversify their investments across a wide range of stocks, bonds, and other funds. In a sense, they would all become personal pension fund managers.

In the technical language of pension economics, GM had replaced its guaranteed defined benefit (DB) pension plan with a defined contribution (DC) pension plan. Like many other companies before it, and many others since, GM "threw in the towel" and went from a DB to a DC plan.

Oddly enough, despite the rather arcane nature of the news, GM's stock, which before the announcement on Monday afternoon was trading around $19.80 per share, jumped up just as soon as the press release hit the newswires. By the end of trading on Wednesday, it settled at almost $21.30 per share. Clearly then, the shareholders and the market liked the news and rewarded GM by bidding up its share price.

Hundreds of companies have made the same move as GM in the last few years, and most of them have been similarly cheered on by the market. Major corporations are basically moving away from providing pension income for life. They are shifting the responsibility to you personally. This is why it is now more important than ever for you to answer this question: *Are you a stock or a bond?*

How Do Pensions Work, Exactly?

At its essence, a traditional defined benefit (DB) pension plan is the easiest way of generating and sustaining a retirement income. When you retire from a DB plan, the employer via the pension plan administrator uses a simple formula to determine your pension entitlement. They add up the number of years you have been working at the company—for example, 30 years—and they multiply this number by an accrual rate—for example 2%. The product of these two numbers is called your *salary replacement ratio*, which in the preceding example is 2% × 30 = 60%. And so, your annual pension income, which you will receive for the rest of your life as long as you live, is 60% of your annual salary measured on or near the day you retired. In the preceding case, if you retired at a salary of $50,000 per year, your pension would be 60% of that amount, which is $30,000 of pension income as long as you live.

Now sure, a number of DB pension plans have slightly more complicated formulas that are used to arrive at your pension income entitlement. The accrual rate of, say, 2% might vary depending on when you joined the plan, how much you earn, and perhaps even your age. In some cases an average of your salary in the last few years or perhaps your best year's salary is used for the final calculation. Some pension plans adjust your annual pension income every year by inflation, whereas others don't, which then results in the declining purchasing power of retirees over time. Nevertheless, regardless of the minutia, your initial income under a DB pension plan is computed by multiplying three different numbers together. The first number is the accrual rate, the second number is the number of years you have been part of the pension plan, and the third and final number is your final salary, or the average of your salary during the last few years of employment. Hence, the term, "defined benefit." Here is the key point: *You know exactly what your income benefit will be as you get closer to the golden years.* This knowledge provides certainty, tranquility, and predictability. This arrangement was the norm for most large North American companies and their employees for more than 50 years. In fact, the earliest defined benefit pension plans have more than a 100-year history.

A defined contribution (DC) plan is the exact opposite of a DB plan and is a broad term that includes self-directed accounts such as 401(a), 401(k), and 403(b). There is no guaranteed benefit, or for that matter, any guarantee at all regarding pension income. As the name implies, only the regular periodic contributions are known and determined in advance. The future benefit that you will receive upon entering retirement is completely unknown. If the stock market, or the particular mutual fund in which your money is allocated experiences a bad month, year, or decade around the time of your retirement, then your nest egg will be much smaller. In general, the responsibility, risk, and yes, the possible rewards, are in the hands of the employee as opposed to employer.

Once again, DC plans contain no formulas or income guarantee. In fact, they don't really focus on retirement income at all. They are salary-deferred, tax-sheltered savings plans, where you and your employer contribute a periodic amount. Your final *retirement nest egg* will depend on how much you (and/or the company) contribute to the plan, how your investments perform on the way to retirement, and what you do with the money when you retire. A 401(k) is a number, not a pension. The amount of money in your 401(k) plan, at the time you retire, is unknown and unpredictable in advance. In the language of probability theory, it is a random number. Indeed, you might experience a bear market just before your retirement date, and the nest egg might lose 20% to 30% of its value, as most plans did during the bear market of 2001 to 2003. The 401(k) plan is, therefore, not a pension. You, the retiree, have to figure out how to convert this into some sort of pension—similar to the defined benefit pension I described previously—as you transition into retirement.

I don't mean to single out GM, because it is not the only company taking this course of action. Indeed, it is difficult to miss the evidence of the decline of traditional private-sector defined benefit (DB) pensions. Countless company press releases, government studies, and scholarly reports have been documenting that DB plans are being frozen, replaced, and converted into defined contribution (DC) plans such as 401(k), 403(b), and other hybrid structures. This is the new reality of personal finance. The responsibility is shifting to you.

The Continued Decline of DB Plans

Like General Motors, companies like Lockheed (October 2005), Motorola (December 2005), Verizon (December 2005), IBM (January 2006), Sprint Nextel (January 2006), Dupont (August 2006), NCR (September 2006), Whirlpool (November 2006), and Citigroup (November 2006) have all taken similar actions. These companies— and many more—no longer offer a traditional defined benefit pension to their new employees. In many cases, they have frozen or terminated the pension accruals for existing employees as well as new employees, which means that even current members of the pension plan will no longer be entitled to any more credit-years beyond those they have already accrued.

To put this trend in perspective, a recently released survey by the Employee Benefits Research Institute (EBRI) claims that one-third of all pension plan sponsors in the U.S. with "open" plans—that is, pension plans that still accept new members—are thinking about freezing their DB plan in the next few years. From a different perspective, according to Watson Wyatt, way back in 1985 a total of 89 out of the largest 100 companies in the U.S. offered a traditional DB pension to their newly hired employees. The vast majority offered traditional pensions. By 2002, this number dropped to 50 out of 100 companies, and in 2005 it was down to 37 out of 100. My hunch is that when the 2008 figures are released, this number might be in the single digits.

Let me stress, though, that very few of these companies are in any financial distress, contemplating bankruptcy protection, being liquidated, or filing for protection from creditors. Many of the previously listed companies are quite healthy, successful, and growing entities that have decided to simply throw in the towel and abandon DB pensions. Why exactly have they shifted this responsibility to you?

Well, one of the main factors that has been contributing to this accelerating pension trend is something that we actually should all be thankful for—namely good health and increased longevity. We are living much longer than anybody anticipated or planned for when these defined benefit pension plans were originally designed and set up more than 40 years ago.

As you can see from Figure I.1, back in the 1970s life expectancy (at birth) was approximately 67 years for males and about 75 years for females. The average of the two was slightly above 70 years. But, in the last 40 years this number has marched steadily higher so that by mid-2007 the average life expectancy was approximately 77 years. This is a 5-year gain within 40 years. Now just think about what life expectancy might look like in 40 or even 80 more years. And that's not the full story because these numbers only apply at birth. As you age the life expectancy numbers get better, not worse. People are living into their hundreds. In fact, General Motor's oldest "pensionsaire" was 110 in 2006.

A few decades ago, pensions were small sums of money paid for a few years between a formal retirement date and the end of the human lifecycle. But now, this period that was intended and estimated to be 5–10 years is turning into 20 or 30 years. People are retiring earlier (with full benefits) from their pension plan and living into their late nineties.

The resulting pressure on the pension system and plans is an unsupportable retiree-to-active workers ratio. There are just too many retirees and not enough active workers, and therefore not enough revenue to go around to continue to support these payments. Table I.1 shows evidence of this trend for the automotive industry. It's becoming too expensive to pay people for the rest of their lives.

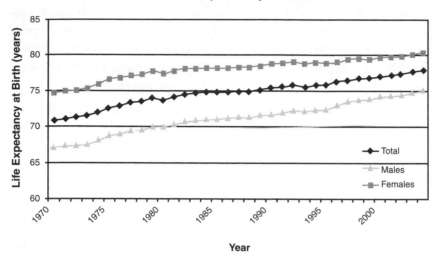

Figure I.1   Up, up, and away.

Source: U.S. Census Bureau, Population Division Working Paper No. 38.

**TABLE I.1   U.S. Auto Industry Retirees Versus Active
Workers**

Company	Retirees Per 100 Workers (median value)
Toyota	2
Honda	5
Nissan	11
Chrysler	153
Ford	163
GM	320

Sources: Eduardo Porter, "Makers Put Health and Pension Burdens
Squarely on the Workers," New York Times, May 19, 2006; GM Letter to
Stockholders, 2005; "GM, UAW Deal May Presage 'New U.S. Auto
Industry,'" Detroit Free Press, 2007; IFID Centre calculations.

Toyota has only two retirees per 100 active workers. Within the
U.S. Toyota is a young company with little if any legacy costs or
longevity risk exposure. In contrast, companies like Ford, Chrysler,
and GM have hundreds of retirees per 100 active workers. After

absorbing the implications of Table I.1, you will appreciate the joke that has been circulating among actuaries in the pension industry that "General Motors (aka Generous Motors) is not really a car manufacturer, but a pension fund and health-care provider for its retirees." Yet, this is no laughing matter. In 2006, GM paid more than $30 billion in pension and health-care benefits. That's what happens when you have more than three times as many retirees as active workers. Now do you understand why GM froze its plan?

Notice from Table I.2 that the ratio of the number of retirees per 100 workers is higher for the U.S. population as a whole than it is for Toyota, Honda, and Nissan (refer to Table I.1), whereas the ratio is greatly reversed in comparison to Ford, Chrysler, and General Motors. Note how the number of retirees per 100 workers is projected to creep up as we move into the middle part of the century. Who will pay for these retirement benefits? How high will these ratios get?

TABLE I.2   Number of U.S. Retirees Per 100 Workers

Year	Number
1950	6
1970	27
1990	30
2010 (projected)	32
2030 (projected)	46

Data Source: Social Security Administration, "The 2007 Annual Report of the Board of Trustees of the Federal Old-Age and Survivors Insurance and Federal Disability Insurance Trust Funds," p. 48.

The editorial displayed in Figure I.2 of the *Financial Times* newspaper sums up the situation quite well.

Consequently, in the last 10 to 15 years, the U.S. has experienced a remarkable shift in the way retirement is being saved for and financed. A mere 15 years ago, the total percentage of "retirement assets" (broadly defined) sitting within traditional defined benefit (DB) plans was close to 25%, similar to the percentage in defined contribution (DC) plans. Yet, today, the percentage that is comprised of DB plans is less than 15%. As you can see from Figure I.3, the direction of the trend-line is quite clear.

Figure I.2   The verdict is in.

Source: *Financial Times*, May 25, 2005.

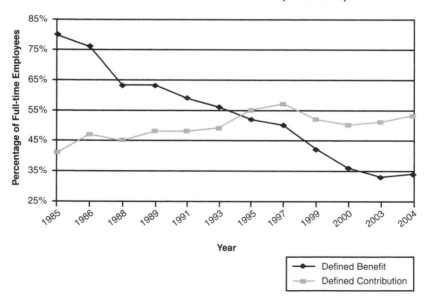

Figure I.3   The responsibility is in your hands.

Source: Social Security Administration, "Defined Contribution Pension Plans and the Supplemental Security Income Program, " March 2006.

No matter how you look at it, one would be foolish to assume this trend of reduced DB coverage in the private sector will halt or reverse anytime soon. The only question is the magnitude and speed.

In fact, some consumer advocates and free-market economists argue that this trend away from the traditional pension system is actually a positive change. The idea is that the increased flexibility, mobility, and clarity of defined contribution plans are more in line with the needs of today's more mobile labor force. For this growing group that plans to be with more than one employer over time, the 401k, or any defined contribution plan for that matter, is the only option.

But, Are the Shareholders Happy?

Using extensive data on pension freezes, I have found that since December of 2001, an average of 1–2 publicly traded companies per month announced intentions to freeze or shut down their DB plan and either replace it with a DC plan or enhance their existing DC plan with better products, more choices, and greater matches. In addition to the companies I mentioned earlier, HP, Wendy's, Nortel, and Nissan are just a few of the major household-name companies that froze their plans between 2005 and 2007. The bottom line was that over a window of ten trading days before and after the announcement of a pension freeze or close, the average increase in stock price was approximately 3.96%. Relative to the SP500 index (or in risk-adjusted terms), the effect was even greater—approximately 4.2%. If we expand the event window to twenty business days before and twenty business days after, the aforementioned impact increases to almost 7.3% in risk-adjusted returns.

My hypothesis for the likely reason is the capping of risk and not necessarily the reduction in compensation expenses or costs. Companies have taken this unquantifiable longevity risk off their corporate balance sheet and transferred it to the employees' personal balance sheets.

I think this further reinforces the important financial fact for 21st-century retirement planning. Soon, very few groups of new employees entering the labor force will be able to rely on a DB pension plan to provide retirement income. Whether you are on the verge of retiring, or think you are much too young to even think that far into the future, the responsibility of generating income in your retirement will more than likely rest in your hands. As part of your holistic personal risk management strategy, this book will motivate you to start thinking about how you and your loved ones will help convert the 401(k) and the sum of money you have saved in your retirement nest egg into a true pension that provides a retirement income that you can't outlive.

The Florida Pension Experiment

Public sector employees who are part of state or local government plans are not entirely immune to the trend I've described. If you live in Florida, you might know this already. Between mid-2002 and ending in mid-2003, every one of the approximately 625,000 government employees who were members of the state's pension fund were presented with a unique decision. Basically, each existing and new employee was granted the option to switch from a traditional defined benefit *pension plan* to a self-managed *investment plan*. In other words, they could take the lump-sum value of their retirement pension, and instead invest the proceeds themselves in a wide range of carefully vetted mutual funds. Alternatively, they could choose to maintain the status quo and remain in their current traditional defined benefit (DB) pension plan until retirement.

The upside or gain from pension switching was twofold. First, the employees would be given the chance to manage and invest the money that they have already earned and accrued, and they will be given the opportunity to do the same with any future contributions. Again, this "investment plan" is not a pension plan. It is a tax-sheltered investment account that will (hopefully) grow over time, the investment returns will (hopefully) beat inflation, and the nest egg will provide a nice cushion for their retirement. However, at some point the employee is going to have to turn this money into an actual pension that provides a respectable income for the rest of his retirement.

So, here are the fundamental questions that permeate much of what I will be discussing in this book:

- Would you take a lump sum in lieu of a pension and invest it yourself, together with all the contributions you would receive from your employer over the next 20 years? Or would you say, "no, thanks" to the offer and just wait until retirement and take a pension based on your 35 years of service?
- If you did decide to take the lump sum and invest it yourself, how exactly would you allocate the money over the next 20 years?

Although I don't live in Florida I, too, face a similar decision at retirement. I am in a defined benefit plan that gives me the option to cash-out in retirement and manage the funds myself for the rest of my life. Luckily I have about 25 years to decide. How about you? Do you think you could manage and invest a nest egg yourself and grow the money to an amount that would generate a greater lifetime income compared to a pension? What if you live much longer than you expected? What if the market declines just when you are about to retire? What if inflation is higher than expected? It's a tough decision, no question! And yet, if demographics and corporate trends are any indication, many millions of Americans will be making this exact choice over the next 5 to 10 years. They have a number—an amount of money in a tax sheltered savings account—and must decide how to convert it into a pension.

Agenda for Book

My objective is to get you to think differently about the many decisions you make on a daily basis, and to highlight the financial and investment aspects of those decisions. The reason this type of thinking has now become more important than ever is precisely because of the very large responsibility that has now shifted into your hands, namely the concern of creating a sustainable income for the rest of your very long life. My bias, if I do have one, is to move people away from short-term investing-by-speculating to a more prudent long-term investing-by-hedging or investing-by-protecting. What risks do you really face over the long-run of your financial life, and how do you manage all of your economic assets to protect against those risks?

For now, unfortunately, many individuals make financial decisions thinking they can outguess the market, their opponent, or nature. The truth is that few if any of us are endowed with this ability. And while it's perfectly fine (and fun) to spend a few thousand dollars betting on whether a given penny stock, mutual fund, or economic sector will outperform another penny stock, fund, or sector, this technique is not the way to manage your personal pension, which must last for the rest of your life. I touch upon this theme—call it the "stop speculating and start hedging" theme—in a number of places within the book.

As you contemplate the possibility of a 30-year or possibly longer retirement, it is very important to start thinking about managing your financial capital more effectively over your lifecycle. This is more than just about creating a pension or sustainable retirement income. It is about proper risk management practiced by major corporations, applied to your personal life. And so, the next few chapters will be devoted to personal financial risk management early in life, which can then prepare you for prudent risk management later in life. Of course, on the way to creating a secure pension, I must start by examining precisely how to measure the value of your own net worth. I will first introduce you to the concept of human capital and why it is likely the most valuable asset you currently own or have on your personal balance sheet. With that in hand, I then move on to discuss very carefully how you should think about risk and return over very long horizons and to understand the role of hedging versus investing or speculating when it comes to managing our human capital. Then, after I get the preliminaries out of the way, I discuss how to properly convert and manage the risk of going from a number in your 401k or IRA plan to a pension that will last for the rest of your life. With the decline of traditional DB pensions, retirement income planning is more than just having the right mix of investments or saving enough in your 401(k) plan. A large sum of money in an investment plan—however you define large—doesn't guarantee you a secure retirement. The strategy you employ and the products you purchase with your nest egg will be more important than the size of that nest egg.

Endnotes

The impact of announcing DB freezes and closures on the stock price of the sponsoring company was studied and documented in the article by Milevsky and Song (2008). For a more extensive discussion of some of the concerns or possible problems with 401(k) plans, see Munnell and Sunden (2003). For additional statistics on the extent of a possible retirement income crisis, see Salsbury (2006), and for a more extensive discussion of the public policy implications of entitlement programs, see Kotlikoff and Burns (2004). Also, the edited books by Aaron (1999) and Clark, et al. (2004) contain some very interesting articles and studies on broader aspects of retirement income planning. Lowenstein (2005) has written an excellent article on the demise of DB pensions from a historical and current-events perspective. The collection of articles in Mitchell and Smetters (2003) provide a more academic perspective on the topic.

1

You, Inc.

"...I am technically broke because I have little money in the bank, I owe money on my credit cards, and I have no retirement savings...."

Myth #1

Let's go back to the very beginning of financial life and let me introduce an entity called You, Inc. This is a small, tightly controlled, privately held company with the bulk of its productive assets invested in nontraded units of your future salary and wages. Your objective as CEO, CFO, and chairman of the board is to maximize shareholder value of You, Inc. while minimizing the financial risks faced by the corporation.

In fact, the financial and risk management strategies plotted in corporate boardrooms of large businesses can be applied to the management of your daily finances. Like any corporate executive, you must take a long-term view when making financial decisions, but at the same time, you have to monitor and control the risks that You, Inc. faces over your entire lifecycle.

The Wall Street Journal doesn't report on the activities of You, Inc. very often, but its corporate history is well known: You, Inc. started life as a subsidiary of a larger company called Parents, Inc., and, for much of its first two decades, You, Inc. was an asset (or liability) on Parents, Inc.'s balance sheet. In purely financial terms, Parents, Inc. likely found You, Inc. to be a poor investment: According to conservative estimates, parents spend at least $100,000 on a child during the first 18 years of his or her life, and may never see substantial dividends. Consequently, the board of Parents, Inc. tends to anxiously look forward to the day when it can spin You, Inc. off into a separate entity.

As the human lifecycle continues, You, Inc. will eventually consider merger opportunities, otherwise known as marriage. Marriage is the largest merger and acquisitions (M&A) activity undertaken by You, Inc., and may occur more than once. Most business mergers usually have a breakup fee attached to the deal. This is meant to protect the interests of the larger and more established company, in the event things go sour prior to consummation. Modern marriages have adopted similar, albeit longer dated, provisions under the ominous name of prenuptial agreements. Once again, this contract is meant to protect the economic interests of the party that stands to gain the least from the merger. In fact, many a merger in the human capital industry of which You, Inc. is part have been scuttled over the meager terms of such agreements.

After the assets are successfully combined and management cultures reconciled, the enlarged You, Inc., which is perhaps now rightfully called Family, Inc., usually looks to acquire new headquarters. Besides the productivity potential of your human capital, your home is your second largest asset. But the investment in a home is undiversified and illiquid, because it can't be sold off piecemeal; hence it can be considered riskier than most publicly traded investments like stocks and bonds. Millions of homeowners who are currently facing foreclosure on their homes because the value has dropped under the amount of debt they owe on the house are experiencing the fact that your personal residence is not a risk-free investment. Like education and college tuition, the purchase of a house is usually financed with debt, a deal that requires the best of your CFO skills. Each of the myriad loan and mortgage options has its own risks and rewards. But as every good CFO knows, speculating on the direction of interest rates is an ill-advised endeavor. The choice between long-term fixed or short-term floating debt, as well as the maturity of the "bond" (the mortgage), depends on corporate needs, tax considerations, and budgeting issues. If, for example, your budget can allow for potential spikes in fluctuating payments, you are better off with a variable or adjustable mortgage, but if cash is tight, fixed is the way to go.

The global push toward shareholder activism has not gone unnoticed within You, Inc., and the various stakeholders, such as children, spouse, and in-laws, will eventually push for a place in the corporate boardroom. You might be the largest single shareholder, but your family members are minority shareholders with protected rights. If anything should happen to jeopardize your lifespan or future productivity, they would suffer grave financial consequences. Prudent risk management dictates that you purchase a variety of insurance policies to protect your largest asset, as well as other investments, projects, and assets you couldn't afford to lose. Practically speaking, the median 30-year-old with $600,000 to $800,000 worth of future earnings would be well advised to buy a similar amount in life insurance.

As your life cycle continues, You, Inc. will likely have some spare cash, and you face difficult dividend-policy choices. A vocal (and likely teenaged) minority on the board might be pushing for big jumps in dividends. However, a savvy CEO will lean toward retaining the earnings because You, Inc. is likely saddled with severe credit constraints and needs to fund future growth.

Because You/Family, Inc. is not a publicly traded company, it can't tap the capital markets to finance new investment projects. After all, you have little in the way of hard assets to pledge as collateral until much later in the life cycle, and financial institutions tend to frown on purchasing shares in You, Inc. on account of slavery being illegal. That leaves you with the option of using internal cash (that is, personal savings) or the much costlier alternative of borrowing from the bank. For many, credit cards are the last (or at least most convenient) resort. But, with effective credit card interest rates being stratospheric, it's hard to find a use for that borrowed money that's worth the cost.

The preceding analogy might be pushing the limits of reality, but I believe the underlying idea, that you should think of yourself as a company and manage your financial affairs using similar techniques, leads to a number of practical insights and takeaways. Thinking like this can help you make better financial decisions. I will get to them later in this chapter and the book, but at this point I would like to go back to the first principles and ask, "What is You, Inc. worth?"

What Are You Worth?

Although I can't answer this question for you personally, I can give you a look at a snapshot of the finances of the typical U.S. household, which I have called "Family, Inc." I can do so using comprehensive data from something called the Survey of Consumer Finances (SCF) conducted by the U.S. Federal Reserve Board. This survey provides a very comprehensive picture of various financial aspects of the personal balance sheet, and I will start with the tangible assets (aka, the left side of the personal balance sheet).

The numbers are slightly out of date because these surveys take time to complete, but in 2004 the typical U.S. family unit had median assets of $173,100, which represents a growth of 21.1% in real (inflation-adjusted) terms since 1998. This median number means that if we were to rank the assets of "richest" to the "poorest" American family, the halfway point would be $173,100. This means that 50% of families have more assets and 50% of families have less. Now, remember, assets don't necessarily imply wealth. If you have $173,100 in assets and exactly $173,100 in offsetting debt, then you have zero equity or net worth and have no real wealth. So for now, let's focus just on assets of the typical American and then later we can get to the debts and family net worth.

The total assets reported in the SCF can be further subdivided into financial and nonfinancial assets; and Table 1.1 shows the median market value of the financial assets that Family, Inc. has accumulated. U.S. family assets include transaction accounts, such as checking, savings, and money market deposit accounts and low risk certificates of deposit. Assets also include tax-sheltered retirement assets such as IRAs (or individual retirement accounts), pooled investment funds (including hedge funds and real estate income funds), and the cash-value of life insurance policies. Other assets include trusts, annuities, managed investment accounts, futures contracts, and loans made to others. There should be no surprises here. In fact, you might recognize your own personal balance sheet as having very similar assets.

Table 1.1 allows us to imagine a typical American family that is in their early forties. They have a checking account and a money market mutual fund account collectively valued at $3,800 and retirement assets of $35,200, which they have accumulated through their work pension plans. They have accumulated $6,000 in tax-deferred savings within an insurance policy, something I discuss further in Chapter 3, "Diversification over Space and Time." They have invested a large portion of their financial capital—$65,000—in government, corporate, and foreign bonds, and $15,000 in publicly traded stocks. In fact, you should construct your own personal balance sheet listing of assets, which is an important exercise to do on an annual basis. It should look similar to Table 1.1.

TABLE 1.1 Financial Assets of Family, Inc.

Type of Asset	% with Asset	Median Amount	Change from '01
Transaction Account	91.3%	$3,800	**–9.52%**
CDs	12.7%	$15,000	**–6.25%**
Savings Bonds	17.6%	$1,000	**–9.09%**
Bonds	1.8%	$65,000	+35.7%
Stocks	20.7%	$15,000	**–29.6%**
Pooled Investment Funds	15.0%	$41,000	+9.92%
Retirement Accounts	49.7%	$35,200	+13.9%
Cash Value in Life Insurance	24.2%	$6,000	**–43.9%**
Other Managed Assets	7.3%	$45,000	**–39.7%**
Other	10.2%	$4,000	**–16.7%**

Data Source: U.S. Federal Reserve Consumer Finances Survey 2004, Table 5 04; IFID Centre calculations.

Table 1.2 moves on to the nonfinancial assets and illustrates that the median family has various personal use assets, which they might consume or use in their daily lives. The most common nonfinancial asset is a vehicle. If we think in terms of medians, they would have purchased a new car less than two years ago, and its current market value is estimated at $14,000. The house they reside in is valued at $160,000 and they have a vacation property that they've recently acquired for $100,000. According to Table 1.2, approximately 11.5% of American families have equity in a privately held business. The median value of this business holding (for those who own this type of asset) is $100,000.

Once again, this is as good time as any to encourage you to sit down and create a similar list of all your financial and nonfinancial assets. There is very little point in creating a long-term financial plan without having a detailed snapshot of your current assets. At the very least, the type of information contained in Tables 1.1 and 1.2 will enable you to benchmark yourself relative to the population as a whole. Remember, though, we will return later to one asset class that is missing from both tables— the value of your human capital. For now, let's stick to the traditional accounting numbers.

TABLE 1.2   Nonfinancial Assets of Family, Inc.

Type of Asset	% with Asset	Median Amount	Change from '01
Vehicles	86.3%	$14,000	–2.78%
Primary Residence	69.1%	$160,000	+22.1%
Other Residence	12.6%	$100,000	+17.4%
Equity in Nonresidential	8.2%	$60,000	+13.9%
Business Equity	11.5%	$100,000	–6.10%
Other	7.5%	$15,000	+17.2%

Source: U.S. Federal Reserve Consumer Finances Survey 2004, Table 8 04; IFID Centre calculations.

Either way, I have reviewed the various assets of You/Family, Inc. The main takeaway, of course, is that almost 50% of families report having money in "retirement accounts" and the median amount of money in these accounts is $35,200. Will it be enough to finance retirement? That is one of the main questions addressed later in the book. For now, let's move on to some other financial metrics and benchmarks.

The pretax "bottom line" of Family, Inc. is shown in Table 1.3. It lists the average versus the median pretax income per family unit, measured over a 15-year period. The average numbers are consistently higher than the median numbers. This is because the median treats all families equally, whereas the average places a greater weight on the wealthier families. It is important to keep this distinction in mind. Remember that the median "value" of the three numbers {1,10, 88} is exactly 10 units. It is the halfway mark. However, the average "value" is a much larger 33, because if you add these three numbers together and divide by three, you get 33 units.

Either way, in 1989, the family unit earned an average income of almost $60K (in year 2004 dollars), and by the year 2004 it increased to more than $70K. This is obviously good news—the sign of a growing corporation.

TABLE 1.3 Pre-Tax Incomes Per Family Unit in Constant Dollars

	1989	1995	2001	2004
Average	$60,100	$55,000	$73,600	$70,700
Median	$38,800	$37,800	$42,700	$43,100

Source: U.S. Federal Reserve Consumer Finances Survey 2004, Table 1 95-98, Table 1 01-04.

Of course, the opposite of all the assets listed in Tables 1.1 and 1.2, which occupy the left side of the balance sheet, are Family, Inc.'s liabilities on the right side. Remember that accountants traditionally place the assets of a corporation on the left side and the liabilities plus "equity capital" on the right side. I'll get to a picture of that in a moment.

Indeed, whether one wants to buy a brand-new car, finance a graduate degree, or purchase a new home, in North America we have access to a number of credit and lending sources that allow us to make such purchases today even if we do not have sufficient financial assets to do so. I discuss the merits and pitfalls of debt in much greater detail in Chapter 4, "Debt Can Be Good at All Ages," but now let's look at what people are actually doing. It seems people hold debt in a number of forms and use it to accomplish numerous goals. So what do Americans owe? How does the level and composition of this debt evolve over the life cycle?

About 76.4% of the population carries at least some form of debt, and the median total debt equaled $55,300 in 2004, according to the most recently published U.S. Federal Reserve Consumer Finances Survey. This is an increase of 34.2% since 2001.

Table 1.4 focuses in on Family, Inc.'s liabilities. Unquestionably, the most prevalent and the biggest type of debt on Family, Inc.'s balance sheet, which has increased significantly in recent years among the population, is its outstanding mortgage. The 47% of families with this type of debt are carrying a balance of $95,000. A mere 4% have other forms of home-equity credit in the amount of $87,000.

TABLE 1.4   Liabilities and Debts of Family, Inc.

Debt Type	% with Debt	Median Amount	Change from '01
Home Mortgage	47.9	$95,000	+27.3%
Other home secured debt	4.0	$87,000	+104.2%
Line of Credit	1.6	$3,000	-28.6%
Installment Loans	46.0	$11,700	+13.6%
Credit Card	46.2	$2,200	+10.0%
Other	7.6	$4,000	+25%

Source: U.S. Federal Reserve Consumer Finances Survey 2004, Table 11 04; IFID Centre calculations.

Credit card debt, a very widely used source of credit among the U.S. population, is totaled at $2,200 on Family, Inc.'s balance sheet. Note that 46% of the population has this credit card debt. This number only includes families who are not paying off the balance in full at the end of the month. Approximately 8% have other forms of debt with a median amount owed of $4,000. Note that this "other" category is a catch-all that can include wonderful strategies like margin debt (or borrowed money used to purchase investment assets—a concept I discuss in detail in Chapter 4). This category can also include items such as loans against a pension in a current job or against a cash value life insurance policy, or perhaps even an informal loan from the neighborhood loan shark. It seems like Americans have a robust and diversified portfolio of debts. And, while some debts make perfect sense, other types of debt like credit cards and installment loans might raise an alarm bell or two, if the funds are being used to acquire depreciating assets that lose value over time.

Table 1.5 provides the percentage of each age group that holds any of three types of debts: credit cards, lines of credit, or installment loans. As one might expect, reliance on the three types of debt tends to be higher in the early stages of life when net worth is the lowest but major expenditures and purchases are made.

Similarly, Table 1.6 examines the debt data from a more formal corporate accounting perspective. It compares the amount that a family owes relative to the value of their assets. In some sense, the lower the ratio of debt to assets, the more healthy the family, although there are exceptions to this rule, which I will discuss in a later chapter. In families whose major breadwinner is under the age of 35, the amount of debt they have relative to assets is roughly $87 per $100. If you remember the fundamental formula that net worth or equity equals assets minus liabilities, then the typical family under the age of 35 has equity of $13 and debts of $87, which implies a debt-to-equity ratio of almost 7 to 1. Such a high ratio in this stage of life is a good reason to think in a more integrated fashion about debt management.

TABLE 1.5 Debts of You, Inc.—Who Has These Liabilities?

Age Group	Credit Card	Line of Credit	Installment Loan
Under 35	47.5%	2.2%	59.4%
35 to 44	58.8%	1.5%	55.7%
45 to 54	54.0%	2.9%	50.2%
55 to 64	42.1%	0.7%	42.8%
65 to 74	31.9%	0.4%	27.5%
Above 75	23.5%	—	13.9%

Source: U.S. Federal Reserve Consumer Finances Survey 2004, Table 11 04.

TABLE 1.6 Debts Versus Assets of Family, Inc.

Age of Major Income Recipient in Family Unit	Value of Debt Per $100 of Assets
Under Age 35	$87.20
35 to 44	$50.30
45 to 54	$35.30
55 to 64	$13.40
65 to 74	$10.70
Above Age 75	$8.30
All Family Units	**$31.90**

Source: U.S. Federal Reserve Consumer Finances Survey 2004, Table 11 04, Table 8 04; IFID Centre calculations.

I found it quite surprising and perhaps even depressing that 23.5% of people above the age of 75 actually had credit card debt. Think about it. This is almost a quarter of the population of people in their seventies. I actually have no problem with retirees taking on debt to finance their lifestyle, but perhaps a reverse mortgage or other, cheaper forms of debt would be much more cost effective and economical.

One other observation that emerges out of Tables 1.4 and 1.5 is that households seem to be diversifying their liabilities among a number of credit sources that charge different interest rates and maintain different terms. Even though the principle of diversification goes a long way as a portfolio hedging tool, it should not be overextended as it has no place in your debt strategy. In fact this is the one area of your personal finances where your eggs *should* be placed in one basket. To optimize one's debt strategy, outstanding balances in different loan "silos" should be consolidated at the lowest possible rate. This can add up to substantial savings over time.

This brings me to the last and very important number that conveys information about the financial state of You, Inc.—the median net worth. This value also rests on the right side of the traditional balance sheet as "Equity" and simply equals the family unit's assets minus its liabilities. While the median net worth of Family, Inc. was $93,000 in 2004, which represents an increase of 11.9% in inflation-adjusted terms since 1998, Table 1.7 presents some interesting data for the population at large. This table displays the extent to which the family unit median net worth varies with the income percentile of the primary breadwinner. Although this observation is somewhat expected because of increased savings that may accompany higher income, the variation in net worth is quite remarkable. This disparity also highlights the potential benefit of tailored financial recommendations and strategies.

Particularly relevant to our discussion of You, Inc., and the lifelong risk management process that you must undertake, is the question of how net worth changes over the lifecycle. Economists summon the so-called "lifecycle hypothesis," to describe the change in financial net worth or wealth as we age. At young ages we have little financial capital or often a negative net worth. Many people borrow money to invest in their education, such as student loans and the like, and therefore start their financial life cycle with little if any net worth. This changes as we grow older, pay back our debts, invest in housing and other assets that might appreciate over time, and gradually approach the retirement years. While we continue to spend, our growing income allows us to accumulate savings. Our financial net worth peaks at the end of our working years and is gradually reduced as we continue to spend throughout retirement. We try and smooth our spending patterns and standard of living throughout these periods in our lives, and the generalized result is the shape illustrated in Figure 1.1. Remember that this is an economic hypothesis or theory and obviously doesn't imply that everyone behaves this way, nor does it mean that you personally should behave in this manner.

TABLE 1.7   **Median Net Worth (Ranked by Income Percentile)**

After-Tax Income in the Year 2004	Median Net Worth	Real Change from 2001
Less than 20%	$7,400	–11.8%
20% to 39.9%	$34,400	–16.3%
40% to 59.9%	$72,500	+6.72%
60% to 79.9%	$160,000	+6.69%
80% to 89.9%	$313,900	+12.4%
90% to 100%	$922,200	+3.75%

Source: U.S. Federal Reserve Consumer Finances Survey 2004, Table 3; IFID Centre calculations.

Real world data is, in fact, consistent with this hypothesis and is summarized in Table 1.8. Households where the main breadwinner is less than 35 years of age have the low median net worth of $14,200. With each age group, you can see that the net worth figure rises substantially as we work toward our financial goals and retirement. The number peaks just prior to retirement with a median net worth of $248,700 for the age 55–64 age group and falls to $163,100 for the group above the age of 75. In other words, it seems that despite some notable exceptions, many individuals do, in fact, behave according to the axioms of the life cycle hypothesis. Stated differently, if you want to smooth your consumption over the course of your financial life—which makes sense on multiple levels—then your financial net worth will evolve similar to Figure 1.1.

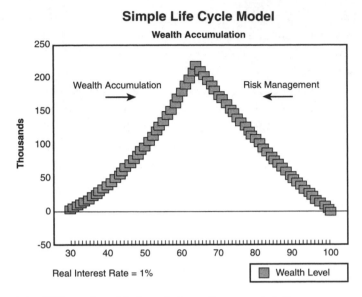

Figure 1.1 Will you be able to get down the mountain?

Source: Life cycle theory and hypothesis based on work by F. Modigliani and R. Brumberg, "Utility analysis and the consumption function: an interpretation of cross-section data," 1954.

TABLE 1.8 Median Net Worth by Age of Household Head

Group	Median (2004)	Real Change from 2001
All Families	$93,000	+0.82%
Less than 35	$14,200	+15.1%
35 to 44	$69,500	**−16.0%**
45 to 54	$144,600	+1.30%
55 to 64	$248,700	+26.0%
65 to 74	$190,200	+0.32%
Above 75	$163,100	−2.06%

Source: U.S. Federal Reserve Consumer Finances Survey 2004, Table 3; IFID Centre calculations.

Let's return for a minute to the early stages of the human life cycle—your late teens and early 20s.

At this age, what was previously a corporate shell becomes an operating unit, and you face the first, and perhaps most important, decision as the head of You, Inc: how to develop and where to invest the company's human capital. "Human capital" refers to your abilities and skills, which you acquire genetically and through education. Through investing in education, job training, and business network- ing, you can build a large stock of human capital that can be mined by You, Inc. for many years, and perhaps generations, to come. Your hu- man capital is converted into financial capital through the earnings and wages you receive during your work career. Hence, we measure your human capital through estimating the value of all your future earnings and wages. The greater your income prospects, the greater your human capital, and the greater the value of You, Inc.

In Table 1.8, the net worth numbers for the median American un- der age 35 tell a bleak tale. Yet one of the main ideas in this book is that when you are young, broke, and possibly in debt, you likely have 30 to 50 productive years of income-generating work ahead of you. Also, although some readers might find the prospect of so many years of work to be depressing, the fact is that the present or discounted value of this income can be in the millions of dollars. This is no differ- ent than any major publicly traded mining company or an oil producer that owns mines and wells that are deep underground and years away from producing any cashflow. It might take decades before they will generate any profits for the company, yet these same companies are allowed to display and value these assets on their balance sheet with the full blessing of financial accountants and securities regulators. Why should it be any different for You, Inc? Thus, I argue that the to- tal asset and net worth values we just examined are understated. As you assess your net worth, the traditional accounting-approach bal- ance sheet should be modified to include human capital along with tangible assets to truly reflect the value of You, Inc. (see Figure 1.2).

Going through the exercise of estimating the present value of your human capital can produce some surprising results—you may find out that you're worth much more in financial terms than you realized. Table 1.9 completes the simple exercise of calculating the value of a 30-year-old's human capital, assuming he will work for another 30 years and earn an inflation- and tax-adjusted salary of $40,500. The value of his human capital is the sum of 30 years worth of salary, dis- counted back to the present day. Obviously the resulting figure varies with the chosen discount rate, which is a subjective number that depends on the stability of the income stream. Yet in all three scenarios in the Table 1.9, human capital is worth more than 90% of the 30-year-old's total capital. That is my main point. Regardless of how safe and predictable or risky and unstable your salary appears, when you have 20 to 30 years of work ahead of you, the discounted value of this asset is likely the largest single item on your personal balance sheet. Of course, your local bank or insurance company doesn't send you a monthly statement that lists or calculates the value of your human capital, but that doesn't mean it isn't valuable.

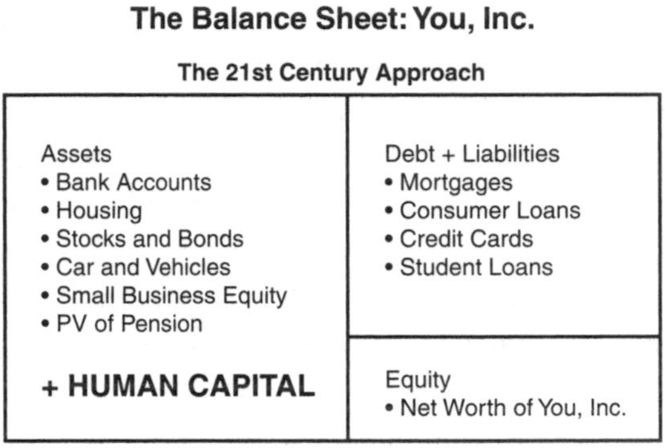

The Balance Sheet: You, Inc.

The 21st Century Approach

Assets • Bank Accounts • Housing • Stocks and Bonds • Car and Vehicles • Small Business Equity • PV of Pension	Debt + Liabilities • Mortgages • Consumer Loans • Credit Cards • Student Loans
+ HUMAN CAPITAL	Equity • Net Worth of You, Inc.

Figure 1.2   We reach the main point—human capital.

Source: Moshe Milevsky and the IFID Centre, 2008.

TABLE 1.9   Example of the Discounted Value of Human Capital

Discount Rate	$ Present Value of Human Capital	% of Total Capital
3.5%	744,900	94%
5.0%	622,600	93%
7.5%	478,300	91%

Source: Moshe Milevsky and the IFID Centre calculations, 2008.

Let me repeat this point again because it is crucial for the next few chapters and for most of the book. The single most precious asset on your personal financial balance sheet is not your savings account, your investment portfolio, your jewelry, or even your house. Rather, it is the discounted value of all the salary, wages, and income you will earn over the course of your working life. This asset is called human capital, and though its precise numerical value might be hard to obtain and difficult to calculate, the fact remains that it's the best asset you have until well into your middle ages.

Figure 1.3 demonstrates the evolution of the ratio of this asset to total capital as we age. The figure illustrates that in the years when we think we are worth the least in pure financial terms, we are actually the wealthiest in terms of our human capital. Once again, you are wealthier than you think.

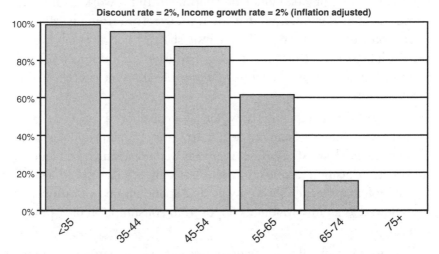

The Ratio of Human Capital to Total Capital for Different Age Groups

*Total capital = human captial + financial capital

Discount rate = 2%, Income growth rate = 2% (inflation adjusted)

Figure 1.3 Even retirees can still work, if they want to.

Source: Baxter, M., "Social Security as a Financial Asset: Gender-Specific Risks and Returns," 1999: IFID Center calculations.

You may be thinking, what good is knowing the value of an asset that you can't immediately use, spend, or borrow against? But I argue that this is precisely the asset that you should take into account when making many of your financial decisions from your initial years of work to beyond retirement. At the very least, get into the habit of computing the value of your human capital each time you get an account statement from the bank, insurance company, or mutual fund listing the value of your financial investments. By doing this exercise, you will get a comprehensive picture of your true net worth and not just a partial view. In many cases, your (limited, narrow) financial investments might have declined in value, but your human capital might have increased by much more. In other cases, it will be the other way around. Either way, it is the sum of the financial capital and human capital, together with the value of your house and other nonfinancial assets, that should truly matter for your financial decisions and well-being.

The concept of human capital as a driver and motivator of household economic decisions was popularized by Professor Gary Becker from the University of Chicago, who was awarded the 1992 Nobel Laureate in Economics. Back in 1964 he published a book with the simple title, *Human Capital*, in which he argued the importance of education in promoting economic development. In his work, using U.S. census data, he documented that the rates of return from investing in education were substantial. His analysis showed that not only was it worthwhile to invest time and effort in acquiring and refining one's education, but also it was a key differentiator of economic success in different countries.

His path-breaking analysis, which was considered rather controversial at the time, was one of the first to justify human capital as a legitimate asset class. At the time, many viewed an advanced college or university education as a luxury item that only the rich could afford. What Professor Becker showed was that spending on education was best viewed as an investment as opposed to consumption or expenditure.

So, for example, if you decide to become a brain surgeon, you invest some 15 years of your life, along with the forgone wages during that time, to develop a gold mine of human capital invested in the medical industry. As a newly minted medical resident, you have few financial assets and likely a large debt from financing the education, but the value of your human capital will be in the millions. If, on the other hand, you opt to enroll in a six-month course in auto mechanics, you invest little human capital. Although this investment might lead to positive cash flow relatively soon, it is not associated with much income stability. The rate of return on "cheap" human capital, when you don't invest much time and effort in developing that human capital, should be quite low.

Table 1.10 summarizes the trade-off between spent tuition dollars and additional education, and its consequences. So while you sacrifice time and foregone wages as you study, you ultimately increase the size of your human capital. And, in fact, this increase in the present value of your future earnings may quite easily justify your expenditure on additional years of school. For example, from the analysis in Table 1.11, if you are currently earning $50,000 and decide to invest in a particular graduate degree that costs $80,000, your income will only need to increase by $6,550 or 13.1% to justify this seemingly large expense.

TABLE 1.10 School and Human Capital Analysis

Total Financial Capital =	Financial Capital +	Human Capital
No investment in education (*status quo*)	Earn wages, save time and tuition costs	Salary stays the same and may not grow.
Go back to school	Lost wages, lost time, paid tuition	The present value of human capital is higher than before.

Source: Moshe Milevsky and the IFID Centre, 2008.

Obviously a number of assumptions are built into the numbers displayed in the table, but the general relationship holds true regardless.

TABLE 1.11 By How Much Does Your Salary Have to Increase to Justify Investing in Education?

	Tuition				
Salary	**$20,000**	**$40,000**	**$60,000**	**$80,000**	**$100,000**
$25,000	10.2%	13.1%	16.1%	19.0%	21.9%
$50,000	8.8%	10.2%	11.7%	13.1%	14.6%
$75,000	8.3%	9.2%	10.2%	11.2%	12.2%
$100,000	8.0%	8.8%	9.5%	10.2%	10.9%

Assumptions: 2 years education, 3% wage growth, and 20-year career.

Alas, You, Inc. only has a limited amount of human capital. As shown in Figure 1.4, as your life cycle approaches its twilight and enters the retirement phase, the ability to generate new financial capital using human capital decreases dramatically.

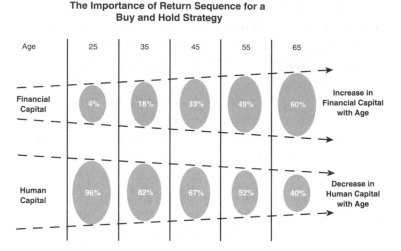

Figure 1.4   A snapshot of your evolving economic life.

Source: Ibbotson Associates (reproduced with permission).

Hence, the ongoing health of You, Inc.'s financial situation depends on converting your finite human capital into financial capital, and ensuring that you grow your financial capital sufficiently to support you and your family when the "gold mine" of human capital can no further be mined.

You will see in the future chapters that the size of this important asset has relevance for numerous investment decisions that you will be faced with throughout your life cycle. The value of your human capital is what you should consider when purchasing life and other forms of insurance, and your human capital's riskiness should be incorporated into all your investment decisions.

Summary

- The typical 40-year-old has almost $50 of debt per $100 of assets. Overall, the typical family unit has $30 of debt per $100 of assets. The median amount of money in retirement accounts is a mere $35,000, and 50% of American families do not have any retirement account. All this implies that many Americans will have to drastically reduce their standard of living at retirement or retire much later than they expected.

- The traditional accounting measures of personal financial net worth and equity, which is computed as the value of assets minus the value of liability.

- Even though you might have very little if any financial equity, you are wealthier than you think. In fact, you probably have an asset worth millions of dollars. It's called human capital. Think of it as the "nest embryo" which will eventually become your "nest egg."

- As you age you convert human capital into financial capital. Your total capital, which is the sum of both types of capital, should be increasing over time.

- Depending on how risky your job is, you may think of your human capital as a stock or as a bond or some combination in between. This analogy will come in handy later, when we talk about comprehensive asset allocation—considering both your human and financial capital—over the life cycle.

- In particular, individuals who expect to receive little or no income from a defined benefit pension plan must be even more careful to manage the conversion of their human capital into financial capital so that they secure a smooth income stream over their entire life cycle.

Endnotes

Modigliani (1986) describes his path-breaking research that led to his Nobel prize, as well as how he developed the life cycle hypothesis. The book by Becker (1993), yet another Nobel laureate, contains a number of his pioneering articles on the economic returns to human capital investment. Bodie, Merton, and Samuelson (1992) wrote the first formal article within financial economics to treat human capital as an asset class that can be primarily treated as a bond. The monograph by Ibbotson, Milevsky, Chen, and Zhu (2007) provides a more technical and mathematical analysis of the value of human capital, in addition to a number of actual case studies and examples that expand on the ideas in this chapter and the next one. Lee and Hanna (1995) wrote another early and relevant paper on how to think about human capital within the context of financial planning. Finally, the book by Lleras (2004) is an accessible book on the international returns to investing in human capital.

2

Insurance Is a Hedge for Human Capital

"...I am young and healthy so I don't need any life insurance, yet. I'll think about it more seriously once I get much older and am more likely to die...."

Myth #2

A few years ago an older MBA student in one of my courses complained to me during a lecture on insurance that he had been diligently paying premiums for years on a multimillion dollar term life insurance policy. With the benefit of hindsight, he was frustrated at all the money he had wasted on the life insurance policy, with no investment return to show for it. I replied, jokingly, that my wife was actually Italian with strong family connections in Sicily, and I might know some people who know some people who might be able to arrange for a large return on his investment; in the style of Tony Soprano.

Life insurance policies, and for that matter, almost all financial instruments that we purchase for risk management purposes, should not be viewed as investments, but as hedging instruments. Oddly enough, the goal for most of these hedges is, in fact, to lose or waste the money. After all wouldn't you and your family rather have you and your human capital, as opposed to the million-dollar payoff? I certainly hope the answer is, "yes."

Nevertheless, to understand the role and pricing of insurance in a more detailed way—and to see how it fits in the "are you a stock or a bond" theory of human capital—in this chapter, I explain how this hedge works in theory and in practice. You will gain a better appreciation for why life insurance is so important when you are young and especially when you have dependents who rely and depend on your human capital. The same ideas apply to disability, critical illness, or any other risk factors that might impede your ability to extract the most value from your human capital, but my remarks will be focused on life insurance.

The Odds of Living and Dying

When you toss a coin, spin a roulette wheel, or shuffle a deck of cards, computing or calculating the probability of getting heads, reds, or spades is straightforward. This is because the underlying "probability distribution" is well known. In fact, regardless of whether the coin, wheel, or deck is new or old, in Las Vegas or Atlantic City, the odds are much the same, and all mathematicians will agree on them.

For example, the probability of tossing two heads in a row is 25% anywhere on planet Earth, regardless of who is tossing the coin. However, when it comes to matters of life, health, and death, the situation isn't as clear. There isn't a well-defined probability distribution from which to calculate the relevant odds. The more a doctor knows about your health, income, and educational level, the better the estimate she can give you; however, it truly is only an estimate.

In the absence of detailed information, all we can do is talk about upper and lower bounds on the probability. For example, knowing only that you are a 40-year-old male living in the United States, one could say that the probability of your dying prior to your 41st birthday is somewhere between 0.10% and 0.26%. We can think of these as optimistic versus pessimistic estimates of mortality rates. If you then tell me that you are wealthier than average, or perhaps less wealthy or healthy, I may skew the number toward the lower or upper bounds. Obviously, countless factors influence how the mortality odds of any one individual look. Your education, ethnicity, health status, habits, and even your marital status all influence your probability of dying in any given year. For example, Tables 2.1 and 2.2 summarize how the level of education influences the mortality of males and females in different age groups. You can see that the probability that a male in the 35–49 age group who has not completed a high school education might be 1.56 more times likely to die in the next year compared to the rest of his age group. Compare this scenario to a male in the same age group who has completed a college education: His probability of dying is only a fraction of the rate that applies to the rest of the group.

TABLE 2.1   Education Versus Mortality: Males

Education	Age 35–49	Age 50–64	Age 65–75
< High School	1.56 x	1.36 x	1.23 x
High School	1.11 x	1.05 x	0.98 x
Some College	0.97 x	0.89 x	0.90 x
College	0.55 x	0.64 x	0.62 x

Source: J.P. Cristia, August 2007, *Congressional Budget Office*, Working Paper #11, "The Empirical Relationship Between Lifetime Earnings and Mortality."

TABLE 2.2   Education Versus Mortality: Females

Education	Age 35–49	Age 50–64	Age 65–75
< High School	1.61 x	1.48 x	1.26 x
High School	1.12 x	0.89 x	0.91 x
Some College	0.78 x	0.82 x	0.81 x
College	0.58 x	0.64 x	0.68 x

Source: J.P. Cristia, August 2007, *Congressional Budget Office*, Working Paper #11, "The Empirical Relationship Between Lifetime Earnings and Mortality."

With all these studies, it is important not to confuse a statistical correlation between two factors, and actual causality. That is, numerous other factors might impact the education-longevity relationship. As an extreme case, a high school dropout who develops a sudden heart condition won't miraculously get better if she completes her GED or re-enrolls in high school. All we can say for certain is that mortality rates are lower among groups of people within the general population who have completed high school and are even lower for the college educated, compared to people who have dropped out of high school. And so, from a practical perspective, if you are a member of the groups identified as having more favorable mortality experience, you should plan for a much longer retirement compared to the average person in the population. Remember that if the mortality rate is lower, fewer people from this group are dying prematurely, which means that they have greater odds of reaching an advanced age of 90 or even 100.

My main point is that the *true* probability of living and dying is never knowable and very much depends on specifics. The best we can do is to rely on generalized estimates.

Sometimes in this book I will select either the pessimistic, optimistic, or moderate estimate and only display that number, just to make a point or to put the number in perspective. Table 2.3 shows the impact of the assumption on the survival chances.

TABLE 2.3   What Are The Chances of Dying During the Next Ten Years?

Current Age	Optimistic Estimate		Pessimistic Estimate	
	Male	*Female*	*Male*	*Female*
40	1.9%	1.0%	3.7%	2.1%
50	4.8%	2.7%	8.1%	5.0%
60	10.6%	6.7%	18.9%	12.2%
70	27.1%	18.0%	39.5%	27.2%
80	56.6%	48.3%	73.3%	59.7%

Source: U.S. Social Security and 1996Annuity 2000 mortality tables; IFID Centre calculations.

As you can see, according to both optimistic and pessimistic tables, the probability of dying during the next 10 years is much higher at age 80 than at age 40. Using optimistic estimates, an 80-year-old female faces nearly a 50% probability of dying during the next 10 years. Effectively, this means that roughly half of the 80-year-old females alive today will not survive 10 years.

A sad thought, but does that mean that an 80-year-old female should have a huge life insurance policy, because she is quite likely to die soon? No, absolutely not! It all comes down to the value of human capital, and not necessarily the odds of death.

To understand why, start by thinking of the way a standard 10-year term life insurance policy works. You pay a relatively small monthly premium in exchange for a very large payout to your beneficiary in the event of your death. The probability of dying during the next few years might be extremely small (say, 1 in 10,000), but the magnitude of loss is enormous, due to the loss of human capital.

Recall from Figure 1.4 that as you age, the value of your human capital is usually converted into financial capital. During your working life, you manufacture wealth and money by spending effort. You want to insure all the effort you will be investing during your working years, which is precisely why you purchase life insurance. Figure 2.1 illustrates this point in a graphical manner.

What Is the Discounted Value of Your Human Capital as a Function of Your Age?

Discounted Value of Human Capital

Value Increasing

30   35   40   45   50   55   60   65

Older ->

Figure 2.1   Crude, but you get the point.

On the horizontal axis of the figure is your age, while the vertical axis shows the value of your human capital. Imagine that you have just graduated from school and are about to embark on a 30- to 40-year career. You have many productive work-years ahead of you, so the discounted value of your human capital is quite high. If you die (or be-come permanently disabled, unable to work, and so on) during your thirties, forties, or fifties, your family and dependents lose many years of your human capital. While the probability of this loss is generally small, the relative magnitude of this financial loss can be enormous and devastating. If these two elements are combined, the need for life insurance falls in the upper-left corner of Figure 2.2, and you should buy insurance to cover this risk.

What Should You Insure?
Compare Magnitude and Probability

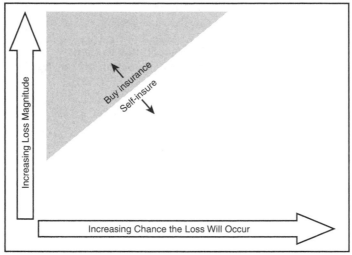

Figure 2.2   Insurance theory—don't waste your premiums.

This might seem like a very cold and detached way of looking at the value of a human life. After all, humans are worth far more than the value of our future wages and pensions. We would give many mil-lions of dollars to bring our loved ones back, much more than what they could have earned or the value of their pensions. But my single most important comment about life insurance is that it is a risk man-agement instrument meant to financially protect your loved ones upon your passing, not to compensate them for the psychological pain associated with your demise. No sum of money can do that.

So returning to the 80-year old female in Table 2.3, whereas her probability of loss (or death) is large, the financial value of her future income (aka human capital) is greatly reduced. Therefore, the relative magnitude of loss is much lower as well, and her need for insurance lies in the lower-right corner of Figure 2.2. In sum, you have to balance these two dimensions and think of them as the critical ingredients of prudent risk management for You, Inc.

How Much Does Life Insurance Cost?

Say that you have assessed your position on Figure 2.2 and have determined that the financial well-being of your family members needs to be protected. How much life insurance do you actually need and what price should you be prepared to pay?

In theory, the insurance premium should reflect the present value of the insurance benefit, adjusted for the probability that the insurance "event" might occur. This is called pricing via the expected present value. In reality, however, price is not so neatly related to the value of insurance benefits for several reasons. First, remember that no product is sold at cost, for zero profit. Your premiums can be, in fact, much higher than what the company expects to pay out, because it is in the business of generating returns for its shareholders. The second reason for the discrepancy is asymmetric information problems between policyholders and insurance providers. This stems from the exact same issue that I mentioned earlier—true mortality rates for two specific individuals are not knowable and the insurance company might be unable to distinguish clearly between high-risk and low-risk policyholders. I might think that a young male driver is likely to take more risks than a 50-year-old woman, but that's a generalization.

Because of this information gap, the insurance company charges a single premium to all policyholders in a certain class; for example, those in a specific age, gender, or geographical group. Typically, the premium charged will be somewhere in the middle of the company's risk assessment analysis. Effectively, low-risk individuals will be overcharged when they purchase insurance, while high-risk individuals will be undercharged. As a result, if buying coverage is optional, then more high-risk consumers will purchase insurance than low-risk consumers. After all, they're getting a bargain. This effect is known as

adverse selection in the language of insurance economists. The insurance company might be taking on more risk than initial estimates of
the population would suggest, because it will have a disproportionate
number of high-risk clients. This could place the company in a potentially ruinous situation, because it will have to pay out more claims
than it expects. Hence, the resulting price-it-in-the-middle approach
diverges from the "fair" price of the insurance—the present value of
expected future benefit payouts.

The bottom line from all this "insurance theory" is that buying any
type of insurance, and life insurance in particular, is more than just a
matter of probabilities. There is a real "game" that goes on between
the buyer and the seller, which impacts the pricing as well. I come
back to this topic later in the book when I discuss the many ways of insuring your investments and your retirement income.

How Much Life Insurance Do I Need?

Although the pricing of insurance is a rather scientific discipline,
determining the amount of insurance coverage that you require is not
as rigorous. Many people mistakenly believe that you can never have
too much insurance. Many in the industry who sell insurance for a living might want you to believe that as well. I disagree. I think that there
is an upper bound (called the income approach) and a lower bound
(called the expense approach), and anything in between is fair game
(see Figure 2.3). By upper bound, I mean the most amount of life insurance that you can possibly justify buying without effectively over-
insuring yourself. By lower bound, I mean the least amount of
insurance you can possibly justify without under-insuring, aka placing
your family and loved ones at risk.

The income approach attempts to estimate how much money you
can expect to earn over the course of your working years and beyond,
which is the value of your human capital. Some practitioners have refined the income approach by subtracting from the previously mentioned number, a fixed amount to take account of income taxes
(because the death benefit is not taxable) and also subtract the expenses you would have incurred had you been alive—this gives you
the amount of insurance you require. Here is a simple example.

Assume that you have estimated the value of your take-home pay over the course of your career, discounted to your current age of 30, and it equals $1,000,000. This is the value of your human capital. A simple application of the previously mentioned income approach would dictate that you purchase $1,000,000 of term life insurance, assuming you have dependents, of course. A more refined approach would be to realize that this $1,000,000 would be received by the family tax-free, and that the family would not incur as many expenses if you are no longer alive (as morbid as this sounds), so you might decide to reduce the $1,000,000 by 20% or so. This is obviously *ad hoc* and not very scientific, but the point is that the income approach provides an upper bound.

Estimating Your Insurance Needs

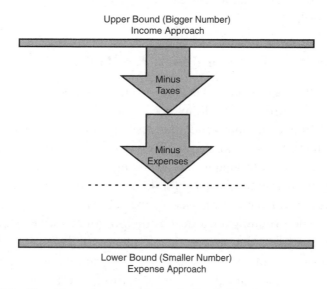

Upper Bound (Bigger Number)
Income Approach

Minus
Taxes

Minus
Expenses

Lower Bound (Smaller Number)
Expense Approach

Figure 2.3   It's not a science, but stay in the ballpark.

The second approach, which usually results in a low amount of insurance, is the expense approach. This method does not focus on the value of human capital *per se*, but instead focuses on the expenses your family will incur over the course of their lives. You then buy life insurance to cover those expenses rather than to replace your income. As you can imagine, a wide variation exists between the amounts of insurance you think you need if you use the (family) expense method as opposed to the income approach. And the wealthier you are and the larger your income, the larger this gap will be.

Here is an example of how the expense approach might work. If you earn $100,000 per year, and you expect this number to remain fairly constant in real terms (after inflation) for the rest of your life, the income approach might lead to about $1,000,000 in life insurance coverage, which arguably could be the present (discounted) value of your wages and salary. The expense approach might compute the costs of living expenses for your family, such as feeding and putting your kids through school, which might only be $500,000. Thus, any number between $500,000 and $1,000,000 would be acceptable as a death benefit on a life insurance policy. Either way, before you get life insurance, sit down with your family members, and possibly an insurance professional, and do an income and expense analysis. The process will be quite revealing.

Can We Put a Value on What a Life Is Worth?

After the tragic events of 9/11, a program created by Congress and headed by retired Judge Kenneth Feinberg was assigned the extremely difficult and unprecedented task of allocating a compensation fund to the families of more than 5,500 dead and injured victims in the terrorist attacks. Although it was a challenge to select the appropriate process, ultimately, a human capital-like measure was used to allocate the funds, in which it was the victim's expected income that had a critical role in determining the award by the program. The average award that was paid for each income level category is listed in Table 2.4. Again, no award, of course, would have been sufficient compensation for the resulting loss and grief. However, this process attempted to arrive at a fund allocation that would be linked to economic loss.

As you can see, although estimating the economic value of a human life is quite difficult, in some cases it must be done. Notice from the table how victims whose salary and wages were higher tended to receive greater compensation compared to those with a lower income. Although some might not consider this to be fair—and strong arguments can be made both in favor and against this policy—the bottom line is the strong link between the value of human capital and one's wages and salary.

TABLE 2.4   9/11 Compensation Fund:
Award for Deceased Victims by Income Level

Income Levels	Average Award
$0	$788,022.03
$24,999 or less	$1,102,135.44
$25,000 to $99,999	$1,520,155.41
$100,000 to $199,999	$2,302,234.80
$200,000 to $499,999	$3,394,624.91
$500,000 to $999,999	$4,749,654.40
$1,000,000 to $1,999,999	$5,671,815.64
$2,000,000 to $3,999,999	$6,253,705.42
$4,000,000 and over	$6,379,287.70
At all income levels:	$2,082,035.07

Source: IFID centre calculations based on Feinberg (2005).

Types of Life Insurance Policies

Finally, when thinking about insuring your human capital, you must decide between two basic categories of life insurance, which go under the odd names of temporary and permanent. The two are quite different approaches to insuring yourself, and understanding the difference in the context of your financial risk management process is important. From a practical point of view, I think it is important to have a combination of both types of insurance and to vary this mix over the course of your life.

Temporary life insurance, which also goes under the name of term life, is a no-frills way of insuring yourself for a specific period of time—for example, one, five, or ten years. Your monthly premiums are guaranteed for the term of the insurance, and at the end of the term, the insurance coverage ends. There are no refunds, cash-backs, or cash-values in your policy. It's like car insurance, home insurance, or an extended warranty one day after the coverage expires. You have nothing. Within the context of life insurance, if you survive to the end of the coverage period, the policy is worthless. Of course, if you die during the coverage period, your beneficiaries will receive the face value (aka the death benefit) of the policy. When the term of the insurance is

over, you might want to get another insurance policy—once you evaluate your needs—for another term, and so the process continues.

Temporary coverage, as its name suggests, is great for temporary
needs. For example, if you have just purchased a house and financed
it with a large mortgage, you might want some temporary insurance to
cover the liability in case something unfortunate happens to you over
the life of the mortgage. Temporary insurance makes sense for young
couples who have growing children, or if the family would face a seri-
ous financial crisis if something were to happen to the primary breadwinner. Remember, the value of your human capital is considerable
earlier in your life, and you want to protect it. I envision the young
couple having a substantial amount of term life insurance while the
children are young, perhaps eight to ten times their annual salaries, as
per the two approaches I previously described, the income approach
or the expense approach. But regardless of whether you take the income or the expense approach in Figure 2.3, your insurance needs will
change over time. As you move along the timeline in Figure 2.1, the
value of your human capital declines. Likewise, family expenses will
decline as children grow up and leave the nest. Of course, there are
exceptions to these rules, such as more responsibilities, new dependents, and perhaps even a large jump in the value of your human capital. However, as you age and renew your term insurance, the
premiums will increase. Why? Well, the probability of dying increases,
so the insurance company must charge more to cover this risk. In most
cases, there is no justification for buying more and more life insurance
as you age.

When discussing replacement of human capital, I am not only re-
ferring to "official" or explicit income. Stay-at-home parents, home-
makers, and caregivers provide valuable services to the family—
services that are costly to replace. I learned the value of unofficial incomes. Some time ago, my wife, Edna, took a two-day vacation and
left me to care for my three daughters, whose ages at the time ranged
from one to six. I quickly realized how much work the kids could be.
Getting them bathed, dressed, fed, and to school, all with no help—
what a job! When Edna came home, one of the first thing I did was to
contact my insurance agent and buy some more life insurance on my
wife, making me the beneficiary.

In sum, the important characteristic of a term policy is its temporary nature, as well as the fact that it has no savings component. This might seem an odd comment at first, because insurance should have nothing to do with savings. But you will see that permanent life insurance does have a savings component.

What is permanent coverage? This type of coverage sometimes goes under the industry name of whole life, universal life, or level life insurance. There are various types of permanent coverage, but the main idea is that your monthly or quarterly insurance premiums remain the same and also contain a savings component. So if you pay $100 per month, perhaps $60 goes toward the insurance premiums, while the remaining $40 goes to a side savings fund. Practically speaking, your policy contains more than just insurance coverage—it also includes investment value.

Why the savings? With term insurance, your premiums increase each year because the probability of dying increases as you age. In fact, when you are in your seventies and eighties, not only are the premiums prohibitively expensive, but you may not be able to purchase coverage at any price. Level, or permanent, insurance is a system whereby you overpay in the early years to subsidize the later years. Level insurance premiums are higher than term premiums for the first part of your life, while term premiums exceed level premiums later on. This is where the savings come in. Because you are overpaying in the early years, the excess over the pure premiums is being invested in a side fund. In some cases, you can actually control where those excess premiums are invested. As you age, some of the savings will be depleted to make up for the fact that your annual level premiums are lower than what they should be. With these so-called universal policies, you can withdraw, or cash in, the excess savings at any time, so you have access to an emergency fund in times of need.

To summarize the risk management process that you should be taking throughout your life cycle, I offer the following slightly more sophisticated way to think about life insurance and risk management, as shown in Figure 2.4. When you are young, the risk that you and your family face is that your mortality or hazard rate will "spike up" and your family will lose its source of human capital. This is why you purchase a financial security that is "long" mortality when you are young.

By the word *long* I mean that if the mortality rate spikes, the insurance company pays the death benefit to your family. When you are (very) young and have (numerous) dependents, you probably want to have millions of dollars worth of a position that is long mortality, because you want to hedge millions of dollars worth of human capital that potentially could be lost if the family loses its breadwinner. Then, as you age, you reduce the magnitude and size of the long position because (hopefully) your financial responsibilities and commitments start to decline when (hopefully) the kids move out of the house and your family has enough financial capital to protect themselves against the risk of your death and disability. In fact, when you are close to retirement, you might not need a long position in mortality at all, because the family might not have any financial exposure to the demise of your human capital. At that point they should only have the emotional loss.

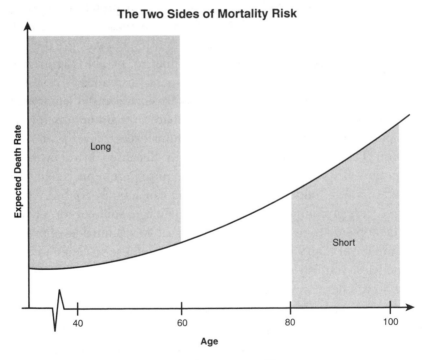

Figure 2.4   Day-trading shares of your mortality.

Source: Moshe Milevsky and the IFID Centre, 2008.

But then, after you are well into retirement, your risk might shift in the other direction. This risk is that your mortality rate spikes down! You now have converted most of your human capital into financial capital, and in all likelihood you have lost your ability to generate any more financial capital. What you do have is a finite nest egg that must last for the rest of your life. The risk you face is that you live much longer than you expected and your nest egg can support. Also, you face the risk—yes, this is a risk—that one of the major pharmaceutical firms develops a drug that extends your life, which again reduces your mortality rate. All of this means you should be "short" and not "long" mortality as you age, and the best way to do this is with longevity insurance and annuities.

I discuss this topic further and in greater detail in Chapter 8, "Spending Your Retirement in Monte Carlo" and Chapter 9, "Annuities Are Personal Pensions," but for now it's important to remember and understand life insurance's role as part of a life cycle financial plan. As you progress through this cycle, your need for insurance must change and adapt. Remember the rate of return on basic life insurance is negative. It is a lousy investment in the traditional sense of generating positive investment returns. However, your human capital is a very valuable asset that should be protected. Although the returns from your insurance policy might be negative, the returns from your human capital are certainly positive. This negative correlation translates to insurance being a great risk management or hedging instrument. In the language of what is often called modern portfolio theory, the correlation between the returns on life insurance and the returns on human capital are quite negative. This is good news for reducing overall portfolio risk, as I will elaborate on in later chapters.

Summary

- The purpose of basic life insurance is to hedge your human capital when you are young and have financial dependents that rely on you for income and support. It is primarily a risk management instrument.
- Basic life insurance isn't meant as an investment. Oddly enough, the best outcome is that you waste all the life insurance premiums and you earn a -100% rate of return.

- In the language of capital market investing, when you are young, you should be "long" mortality risk. If mortality spikes, your dependents get a financial payoff. But, as we shall see later in the book, once you are older, you should go "short" and hedge the risk of a long life. That can be achieved with a pension annuity.

- Later on in life, you reduce the need for life insurance to hedge human capital and mortality risk. You might want to maintain some level of life insurance for estate planning purposes, but that is driven primarily by tax considerations. As you age, the risk management focus should shift to the risk of outliving your wealth.

Endnotes

Some of the material in this chapter is based on the joint research work I did with Aron Gottesman and published in the reference Milevsky and Gottesman (2004). The concept of human capital applied to life insurance was first pioneered by Professor Solomon Huebner at the Wharton School of Business, almost 80 years ago. He called it human life value. For extensive details on the various insurance policies available in the U.S. market, see the book by Baldwin (1994), which provides an in-depth description of their relative merits and benefits. Ostaszewski (2003) delves further into the idea of life insurance as a hedge against a catastrophic loss of human capital. Finally, the recent monograph by Ibbotson, Milevsky, Chen, and Zhu (2007) provides many more case studies and numerical examples, albeit on a more technical level, in which the optimal amount of life insurance is derived and calibrated for given individuals, their risk tolerance, and career characteristics. Much of the work in this chapter is inspired by these references, and I encourage the interested reader to follow up on these sources for more information.

3

Diversification over Space and Time

"…It is a good idea to allocate most of my 401(k) account to my own company's stock, since I can keep an eye on things here and the stock price has been doing really well, lately…."

Myth #3

The famous economist John Maynard Keynes was once quoted as saying that he did not believe in diversifying his investments. He felt that the best investment strategy was to buy a few good stocks, and just hold on to them. In stark contrast, Peter Lynch, the legendary Fidelity Investments guru, is rumored at one point to have owned more than 1,000 different stocks as part of Fidelity's mutual fund portfolio.

Keynes's comments aside (how do you find those few good stocks?), by now it is accepted wisdom that diversifying your investments makes good strategic business sense. The Nobel committee has awarded quite a number of prizes to economists who developed and furthered these ideas about diversification during the last thirty years. Yet, the idea, "Don't put all your eggs in one basket," was a philosophy preached long before the emergence of modern portfolio theory. In fact, the Babylonian Talmud, compiled more than 2,000 years ago, recommends that a person split his wealth into three parts. One-third should be placed in real estate, one-third in money, and the remaining third in business assets, which I liberally interpret to include equities. Overall, not bad investment advice, especially if you could have followed it for the last 2,000 years.

Why does diversification work? After all, wouldn't you think that the more stocks you own, the more likely you are to catch a loser? Or at least that you're as likely to catch a loser as you are to bag a winner? Is it possible to be overdiversified and own too many stocks? And if it is possible, wouldn't these same general issues apply to mutual funds as well? Thousands of mutual funds are available in North America today. Does any one mutual fund have enough stocks in it to be labeled "diversified"? How many mutual funds should you own to be properly diversified? Given the emerging global economy, how much international exposure should your investments have? And finally, now that we have moved beyond the traditional view of the personal balance sheet in Chapter 2, "Insurance Is a Hedge for Human Capital," what adjustments must we make to the diversification concept?

To answer these and related questions on the benefits of diversification, in this chapter I would like to focus on the core reasons for diversifying, and I want to do that by examining the odds the investments you choose go up, go down, or go nowhere. After you understand the exact reasons for diversifying while you are saving for retirement, you can then transition into what exactly happens after you arrive at retirement. My main argument here is that when you are accumulating wealth (but not withdrawing any funds or money from the portfolio), the most important concept you must understand is diversification.

Why Does Diversification Work?

One thing I should make clear about the whole subject of diversification is that nothing is inherently magical about splitting your 401(k) or IRA money into many small parts and putting each part into a different investment vehicle. The benefit is not derived from the process of splitting the money, or placing it into different mutual funds. Rather, it's the simultaneous movement of these investments that's important. In other words, how do they behave, move, and grow over time? Do they move in lockstep? If one zigs, does the other zag? Obviously, these are critically important questions, because if the various investments all move in the same direction at the same time, up or down, you're not likely to benefit very much from diversifying. If they're all moving up, you might as well pick one good fund, or stock for that matter, and stick with it. And if they're all moving down, diversification clearly hasn't helped.

The secret to successful diversification is an old axiom: Opposites attract. In investment terms, that means you want to diversify into sectors of the global and local economy that do not share the same up and down influences. For example, if you invest in both the financial services sector and the consumer products sector, you hope that when one is faltering, the other is not. Or if you further diversify into oil and gas and other resource industries, then ideally, if the first two sectors suffer, the third will prosper. The way to quantify this parallel movement is by using something statisticians label a correlation coefficient, which can range from negative 100% up to positive 100%. The language can be a bit technical, but the concept is simple, so let me explain how the correlation coefficient works, and why it is so fundamental to the investment process and diversification issues.

An Example

To make these concepts a bit more concrete, here's an example that illustrates the effect of diversification and the trade-off involved. Consider three hypothetical mutual funds where one fund exactly tracks or mirrors the performance of the stock market as proxied by the SP500 index, one fund tracks a U.S. diversified Bond Index, and the third fund invests entirely in one-year Treasury Bills (T-Bills). Figure 3.1 graphs the value of an initial $1,000 invested and held in each of the three funds from January 1999 to December 2006, a period that brought a significant stock market downturn at its midpoint.

The initial $1,000 invested in the SP500 Index fund in January 1999 is worth $1,131 in December 2006. Similarly the initial $1,000 investments in the U.S. Aggregate Bond Index fund and T-Bills on January 2000 are worth $1,473 and $1,255, respectively, on December 2006.

While 1999 brought a very favorable return of 21.04% for the SP500, it was also followed by a three-year bear market. Although historically the return from stocks has followed a positive trend in the long-term, by the end of this volatile six-year period, the fund tracking the SP500 lost the race and ended with the lowest balance. With perfect foresight, one would, of course, select the U.S. Bond Index fund to benefit from the higher returns realized over the period.

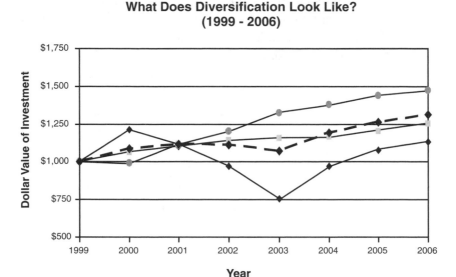

What Does Diversification Look Like?
(1999 - 2006)

Figure 3.1   Predicting the future is very hard.

Note: Diversified fund consists of an equal allocation among the three asset classes.

Source: IFID Centre calculations.

Now, assume you didn't have a crystal ball and that you decided to invest $1,000 in a portfolio consisting of equal weights of these three distinct asset classes; in other words, you diversified your portfolio by investing $333.33 in each. The growth of this investment is represented by the dashed line in Figure 3.1. Now, the $1,000 you invested on January 1999 is worth $1,315 on December 2006. As you can readily see, the final balance of this diversified fund is lower than the balance you would have earned if you had invested in the Bond Index alone. But it is also higher than either the SP500 Index fund or the T-Bill fund. Now here is my main point: Notice the smoother, less jagged path that is followed by the diversified investment. Such is the effect of diversification. With hindsight we might regret not choosing the best performing asset; but while we forego the positive extremes and don't fully realize the returns on high-performing assets, we also avoid the disappointment and volatility of negative extremes.

So regardless of whether you are looking at three or three hundred stocks or funds, there's an implicit trade-off when you diversify. Still, there is universal agreement that diversification is an essential investment strategy. To gain a deeper understanding of why and how the statistical benefits of diversification outweigh the potential gains of investing in a single outstanding stock, you have to consider the risk dimension.

Why Do Prices Move Up and Down So Much?

Generally speaking, when we are considering a given investment asset, the industry assesses the riskiness or volatility of this asset's returns by using something the statisticians call the standard deviation of the asset's returns. This statistic is a measure of how widely the investment returns differ from the average. Figure 3.2 illustrates what this means graphically based on 78 years of return values from the SP500 total return index and long-term bonds. You can see that in the case of the SP500 total return, each return bin or category along the horizontal x-axis contains recorded returns, even if with a low frequency. The returns are widely dispersed, showing a greater probability of achieving very high gains and devastatingly high losses. This is the characteristic shared by all high-risk or volatile investments. Conversely, long-term bond returns over the same period are clustered around the expected or average return for the asset class at the middle of the horizontal axis, with few if any observations in the outer return categories. This low volatility or dispersion is typical of low-risk or low-volatility investments.

Now even more specifically, one must recognize that the risk associated with a stock is really a combination of two types of very distinct risks. One is called general market risk; the other is called individual security risk. Let me briefly explain what I mean by these types of risk, and why it's important to keep track of both.

General market risk, or systemic risk, refers to risk associated with changes to stock prices that have nothing to do with an individual company, but are instead due to changes in the overall economy. For example, if the U.S. Federal Reserve decides to raise interest rates unexpectedly, it will affect the market as a whole, probably in a negative manner. In other words, there will be more sellers than buyers and stock prices will fall. Similarly, if the economy were to slip into a recession, it would affect the entire market, not just a handful of stocks.

A stock whose price changes closely follow the price changes of the market, as proxied by a stock index, contains more general market risk than a stock whose changes are not closely related to changes in the general stock market.

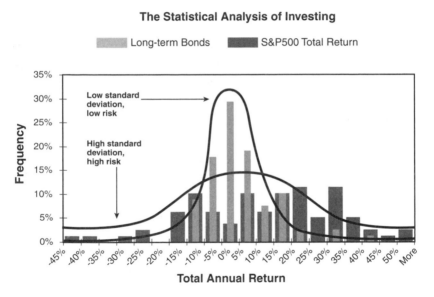

Figure 3.2   Stocks do better than bonds, with time.

Source: Moshe Milevsky and the IFID Centre, 2008.

Aside from general market risk, a company as represented by its stock price also faces risks unrelated to general economic or market risk. Individual security risk, or unsystematic risk, refers to risk associated with changes in the stock price that are due to events associated with the firm itself, independent of changes in the overall economy or the market.

There are numerous potential sources of individual security or firm-specific risk. Sales may decline or rise sharply. The company may fall victim to a fire, sabotage, class-action lawsuit, or accounting fraud.

Alternatively, the company might acquire rights to a proprietary patent or might have just hired a star sales manager or new CEO. All the preceding, as well as their less dramatic parallels in day-to-day operations, can yield stock price changes and volatility entirely independent of the broader market.

Back to my main point here: An essential difference exists between market risk and individual security risk. Market risk cannot be erased by diversification; unique firm-specific risk can. That's because the source of market risk changes in the overall economy. Although a single firm might face a catastrophic event on a single day, it is far less likely that a number of firms will face similar catastrophes on the same day. Hence, the importance of unique risk diminishes as the number of firms in the portfolio increases.

A fundamental axiom of modern financial economic theory is that investors are only rewarded for risks that cannot be diversified away. Individual security risk can be virtually eliminated by holding other stocks in the same industry or sector; general market risk cannot be eliminated by holding more stocks of the same or any industry or sector.

Here's an analogy a student of mine once used to explain this back to me after one of my classes on investment theory. It might sound odd at first, but it makes the point.

One of the more dangerous competitions athletes can participate in is NASCAR auto racing. Clearly, a NASCAR driver with an opportunity to participate in one of the frequent races will evaluate whether the danger associated with racing around a track at 200 miles an hour is offset by the many benefits, including the potential for lucrative endorsements if he or she wins one of the races. Indeed, one can treat the expected value of these benefits as the reward for taking on the risk associated with participating in the NASCAR race. As I said many times, risk and reward are linked.

Now, suppose that a driver has agreed to participate in the Indy 500, for example, but, for whatever reason, has also decided to forgo all the protective gear typically used by drivers, such as protective helmets and clothing manufactured from inflammable materials. Clearly, this driver would be increasing his or her personal risk greatly (and might be prohibited from doing so by the official organizers).

However, is it sensible to claim that these drivers receive extra compensation because of these additional risks? Would a NASCAR driver with no helmet get a better endorsement deal?

The logical answer is no. From a strictly economic point of view, drivers cannot avoid certain risks associated with auto racing. Hence, these risks should be compensated. But if a risk can be avoided, they are not compensated for acting carelessly. Because the proper protection can eliminate or reduce avoidable risk, there is no benefit to assuming such risk.

The takeaway is that diversification of your 401(k) plan has two attributes:

- If you diversify across different funds and companies, you will smooth out the fluctuations and volatility.
- If you don't, you will not be compensated for this extra risk. The fund units and investments will just bounce around, with little to show for it in the long run.

The Importance of International Investing

I have focused so far on domestic stock diversification. In reality, of course, an investor can choose to diversify not only across individual stocks or sectors, but also across different types of investments and more importantly across geographical regions.

Unique risks are associated with individual country markets. Most investors trade in stocks of domestic firms in a particular market. Therefore, if that market were to experience a political or economic catastrophe, the domestic firms traded on the market would all be affected. But these events may have less of an effect on companies and stocks in other countries.

Through international diversification, an investor can avoid the risks associated with a single country. Note, however, that domestic events in some countries can impact international stocks as well. For example, insulating against unique risk associated with powerful economies like the United States or Japan is difficult due to the impact that events in these countries have on other countries in their region or in the world.

Similarly, other types of diversification might be useful as well. Diversifying across different investment asset classes or categories is important. For example, the fixed income asset class is a category that includes savings bonds, government bonds, and other "safe" products that pay coupons and interest. Another asset class is real estate, which can help reduce inflation risk. The value of fixed-income investments decreases as inflation increases. Conversely, the value of real estate increases as inflation increases. A portfolio containing all of these asset classes will be insulated against shocks or surprises to inflation risk.

Diversifying across investments with different levels of liquidity might be useful as well. Liquidity refers to the speed and cost with which investors are able to liquidate all or some of their portfolio, such as when faced with a medical emergency or a family business on the verge of bankruptcy. For example, real estate is commonly perceived as an illiquid investment, due to the time and various fees (agent, lawyer, tax) associated with a purchase or sale. Conversely, money market investments can be quickly and cheaply liquidated.

Consider, for example, two broad stock market indices—for example, in the U.S. and Europe. If you think about it for a moment, you'll see that there are three broad possibilities for how these two markets might behave vis-à-vis one another or move at any point in time. Statisticians call this a positive correlation, a negative correlation, and no correlation.

The first possibility, the positive correlation, simply means or implies that both markets move together in roughly the same direction. When European stock markets are having a relatively strong week, month, or year, then U.S. markets are doing the same. And when European markets are experiencing difficult times, so are the U.S. markets. They share the same ups and the same downs. The stronger (or closer) this parallel is, the higher the correlation coefficient. In fact, if the two markets moved in perfect lockstep, a statistician would say that they have a correlation coefficient of 100%.

On the other side is negative correlation. This means, for example, that when one market does better than average, the other performs worse than average. When one market has a relatively good week, month, or year, the other has a relatively bad week, month, or year. In the extreme, a correlation coefficient of –100% implies that the markets move in exactly opposite relative directions.

Of course, in the new global economy, finding such negatively correlated markets is tough. Indeed, more typically, a rising tide lifts all ships (and vice versa). But if you look hard enough, you should be able to find some market segments that are countercyclical to others. This is why diversifying your 401(k) and IRA investments internationally as well as across asset classes is so important.

Now, just to get a clearer sense of how correlation operates, here is an example. Over the last 20 years, the correlation between U.S. equity returns and European equity returns has been roughly 60%. This means that when the European stock market is having a better-than-average month, the U.S. market is also having a better-than-average month.

Reviewing the last two decades, statisticians have measured the strength of this positive parallel movement on a scale of 0 to 100 and come up with the number 60. This is definitely a positive correlation coefficient, but not necessarily a very strong correlation. Still, it makes a certain amount of intuitive sense that global capital markets should move at least partially in tandem.

So why am I so preoccupied with correlations? Who cares if or how different markets move together? Well, as I suggested earlier, correlation is the key and secret to diversification's success.

Correlations: The Magic Behind Asset Allocation

Think of financial correlation this way. Suppose you are faced with two investment funds. You expect both to make you a few dollars. Moreover, there is a significant additional benefit: The two markets in which you might invest are not perfectly correlated. They do not move together in a parallel direction. Thus, you have a better chance to gain by holding both of them. Let me explain why. Assume that you split your money equally between the two investments. For various hypothetical correlation scenarios, Table 3.1 shows the probability that you will earn less than you would if you invested instead in a one-year certificate of deposit (CD) earning 5%.

TABLE 3.1   Your Money Is Split Equally Across Two Investments: What Is the Probability of Earning Less Than a *One-Year* 5% Certificate of Deposit (CD)?

Correlation Between Investments	Probability of Shortfall
100%	36.94%
75%	35.33%
50%	33.43%
25%	31.11%
0%	28.18%
–25%	24.28%
–50%	18.63%
–75%	9.44%
–100%	0.00%

E[r]=15%, vol=30%; probability each asset earns <5% = 36.94%

Note: Each investment is assumed to earn 15% per year.

Source: Moshe Millevsky and the IFID Centre, 2008.

As you can see, in the most extreme case, when the correlation between the two investments is a perfect 100%, the probability of earning less than the CD is roughly 37%—very high, indeed. If you knew beforehand that there was almost a two-in-five chance that your investment would fare no better than what you could get from a very secure certificate of deposit at your neighborhood bank, you would think twice, wouldn't you?

So it seems that with a perfect, 100% correlation, there are absolutely no benefits to diversification. If you split your money into two baskets that are in exactly the same place (two markets that are perfectly correlated), you have basically kept your eggs in the same basket. By analogy, then, if you diversify into perfectly correlated investments, the odds of earning less than a standard 5% deposit are the same as if you did not diversify.

At the other extreme is the correlation coefficient of –100%. In this case, if you split your money between two investments, the odds of earning less than a 5% CD are reduced to a perfect zero. In other words, you will never do worse than 5%. You have basically taken two risky investments, put them together in your investment portfolio, and created a situation in which you will never lose money. Not bad at all.

Well, of course, I can't guarantee that. Remember, this is purely a hypothetical example in which the correlation coefficient is artificially set to –100%. In the real world, you can never really find such a situation. Think again about the example. If one investment does better than average by x%, when the other performs worse than average by x%, then the good return more or less nullifies the bad return, and you are left with the average. In sum, the perfect negative correlation means that any bad surprises from one investment will be offset by good surprises from the other asset. Put them both together in the same portfolio, and you have no surprises.

Now, you may be thinking that if the two investments are perfectly correlated in a negative fashion, why don't they completely cancel each other out, leaving you nothing at the end of the year? If one completely zigs, when the other completely zags, shouldn't you be left with a flat profile?

Not exactly. Remember that negative or positive correlations are rarely 100%. More importantly, I did not say that when one investment goes up 8%, the other goes down 8%. I said that when one goes up by more than the average performance of the market, the other goes down by more than the average performance of the market.

In Table 3.1, I assumed both investments are expected to increase by 15% per year. The perfect negative correlation therefore means that when one market goes up 23% (8% more than the 15% average expected), the other will increase by only 7% (8% less than the 15% average expected). In other words, one has climbed 8% more than average, while the other has risen 8% less than average. But both have gone up.

Enough with perfect correlations. Let's take a look at the more reasonable and more common middle ground. In other words, let's see what happens when you diversify into investments that have correlations that are much greater than –100% and much smaller than +100%. For example, in Table 3.1, you will see that if the correlation coefficient is exactly zero —that is, there is absolutely no relationship between the two investments' movements—the probability of earning less than a 5% CD is roughly 28%. Compare that with the 37% chance of doing worse than the CD by having all your eggs in one basket.

This is a reduction of 37% – 28% = 9%. In short, by splitting your money into two parts, you are reducing considerably the risk of underperforming the CD. Thus, as you can see, even though the correlation between the two investments is zero—that is, if one does better than average, there is no indication of how the other will perform—there are still benefits to diversifying.

Similarly, if the correlation coefficient is –25%, the odds of your portfolio doing worse than the term deposit is 24% (or about one in four). Compare that with the 28% chance of doing worse when the correlation is zero. Once again, the benefits are clear. The lower the correlation between the two investments, the lower your risk.

I like to call this the fundamental law of diversification: "The risk of the sum is less than the sum of the risk."

What do I mean? Remember that you need two ingredients or factors for successful diversification. The first is nonperfect correlation; the second is an expectation of some profit from both investments. How much you benefit from diversification will depend on the strength of these two factors.

By investing in two imperfectly correlated assets, you are reducing the overall shortfall risk compared to the individual shortfall risks of each asset. Thus, the risk of the sum, which is the risk of the portfolio that consists of two assets, is less than the sum of the risks; that is, just adding the risk of each individual asset.

Let me clarify this point by walking through a detailed example. We know that if you put $100 in a term deposit that pays 5% per annum, you'll have $105 at the end of the year. Not much of a payback, but very safe. Now, let's pretend that you want to invest in the market, take some risk, and diversify. Instead of putting your money in the bank, you put $50 in one asset (let's call it Fund XYZ), and $50 in another (Fund ABC).

Now, we know from Table 3.1 that if there is zero correlation between the price movements of these two investments, then you stand a 28% chance of having less than $105 at the end of the year. This is what I call the risk of the sum. It's the risk of your capital, or the risk of your portfolio.

On the other hand, if you put the entire $100 in any one asset, either Fund XYZ or Fund ABC, the chance of earning less than $105 now rises to 37%. This is what I call the sum of the risk. The fundamental law of diversification in action means that the risk of the sum (28%) is less than the sum of the risk (37%).

An additional point to mention is that in Table 3.1, we are dealing with a one-year horizon. It examines the shortfall odds over a 12-month period. What happens if we extend this correlation analysis to a longer time horizon?

Table 3.2 paints the longer-term picture. This time, the returns on money split equally between two investments (in various correlation scenarios) are compared at five years (with a five-year, 5% compounded CD) and at 10 years (with a hypothetical 10-year 5% CD).

TABLE 3.2   Your Money Is Split Equally Across Two Investments: What Is the Probability of Earning Less Than a _5-Year_ and a _10-Year_ 5% Compounded Certificate of Deposit?

Correlation Between Investments	5-Year Probability of Shortfall	10-Year Probability of Shortfall
100%	22.80%	14.59%
75%	20.00%	11.70%
50%	16.92%	8.79%
25%	13.53%	5.96%
0%	9.83%	3.39%
−25%	5.94%	1.37%
−50%	2.31%	0.24%
−75%	0.17%	0.00%
−100%	0.00%	0.00%

E[r]=15%, vol=30%; probability each asset earns <5% compounded for 5 yrs = 22.80%; for 10 yrs = 14.59%

Source: Moshe Milevsky and the IFID Centre, 2008.

As you can see, Table 3.2 has uniformly lower shortfall probabilities than those in Table 3.1. What does that mean? It means that the odds of earning less than a five-year compounded 5% CD decrease the longer you hold the investment.

But even more important than the time-horizon effect in Table 3.2 is the fact that the amount by which the shortfall risk is reduced depends on the correlation coefficient between the two assets that you are mixing in your portfolio. In other words, the lower the correlation, the lower the risk.

Compare, for example, the zero correlation case. In Table 3.1, looking at risk over a one-year period, the probability of shortfall was roughly 28%. In the case of a five-year horizon with zero correlation between the assets, the probability of shortfall is reduced to roughly 10%. Over 10 years, the same zero correlation between the two investments leads to a shortfall risk of approximately 3%. Isn't it remarkable what four (or nine) more years of investing can do?

The reduction is even more pronounced if you look at a –50% correlation. Remember, a negative correlation means that when one asset is doing better than average, the other is doing worse than average. In other words, they are generally moving in the opposite relative direction. The –50% is midpoint on a scale of –100% to 0% and measures the relative strength of this opposite movement. In Table 3.1, the one-year horizon case, the probability of shortfall is roughly 19%. In Table 3.2, the five-year horizon, the odds are reduced to a mere 2%. For 10 years, it is reduced to less than a quarter of a percentage point. Notice the effect of time and the effect of correlation.

What are the lessons from these observations? Two things will reduce the shortfall risk of your portfolio:

- The longer time horizon over which you hold the portfolio.
- The movement of the assets in your portfolio. The more independently they move, that is, the lower their correlation, the more your risk is reduced.

I like to argue that there are two dimensions to investment diversification—time and space. In other words, there are two aspects to diversification. By time, I mean the length of time you hold the portfolio—the longer you hold it, the more diversified your portfolio becomes. If you consider the essence of diversification to be the reduction of shortfall risk—owing to the imperfect correlation—then holding the portfolio for longer periods of time will also reduce shortfall risk.

I believe that if you invest in U.S. equities during the year 2000 and during the year 2001, you are essentially holding two different investments. Sure, they are the same asset class, namely, U.S. equities. But the returns from these two investments are most likely uncorrelated; that is, the return in one year is independent of the return in the next. If U.S. equities do better than average during 2000, the odds are still only 50/50 that they'll do better than average during 2001. So I would argue that you diversify your investments by holding both equities in 2000 and equities in 2001. You see, in my opinion, the word *diversification* is not just about diversity at any one point in time; it's actually about investing in products that do not move together, so that your shortfall risk (probability of regret) is reduced. Therefore, investing for long periods of time in one asset is qualitatively similar to investing in different assets over one period of time.

By space diversification, I mean that the more independent assets you have in your portfolio (independent in the sense of not moving in tandem with each other), the more diversified the portfolio becomes. I chose the word *space* to reflect this principle because when you diversify across geographic and economic boundaries, you are likely, though not necessarily guaranteed, to find investment assets that move independently.

I do hope you grasp the main point that emerges from this general approach. Specifically, the positive effect of more time (a longer holding period) and more space (more investments that move independently of each other) on your portfolio. Now let me address some of the real-world issues.

Practically speaking, if your investment portfolio is holding only U.S., broad-based equity investments, you are subjecting yourself, in one year, to a 37% risk of not beating a 5% CD. This conclusion comes from the Figure 3.1 one-year, one-fund case. But—and here is the crux—if you can find and invest in another asset class that is expected to increase but is not perfectly correlated with your U.S.-based equity investment, you will gain from the law of diversification. And the less correlated this asset class, mutual fund, or investment is with the U.S. market, the greater will be your gain.

The same diversification principle, of course, is applicable to more than just national stock markets. Bonds, real estate, precious metals, commodities, and even art do not move with perfect correlation to U.S. equity markets. The actual correlations vary over time but there is room for most of these asset classes in a well-balanced portfolio because they will all help to reduce your shortfall risk—the risk of doing worse than the risk-free, 5% benchmark. Remember the two ingredients, though: They must have imperfect correlation and they must have a reasonable chance of making some money over time. (The price of Elvis memorabilia is not correlated with the general stock markets, but I'm not sure about the growth prospects.)

So what, then, is the right amount of diversification for you? Precisely how much should you invest in each of these asset classes? What allocation is the right one given your circumstances? How much should you invest in the U.S., the U.K., Germany, or even Japan?

Good questions. Unfortunately, as is often the case with investment decisions, the answers depend on your personal circumstances, needs, requirements, fears, and phobias—otherwise known as your attitude toward risk. I do not have a cookie-cutter, formulaic answer that will fit all possible contingencies. In fact, I am very much averse to computer programs and black-box solutions to your investment needs. You must discuss these issues with your financial planner, investment adviser, broker, or even tax accountant.

How Does Time Impact Financial Risk and Volatility?

Imagine that you've just received a windfall inheritance from a distant relative. You decide to pay off some bills and, having done so, you discover that you still have $10,000 left over. You don't really need the money right now, so you decide to put it away for a rainy day.

You call up your financial adviser and ask, "What should I do with the $10,000? Should I put it all into a well-diversified index fund? Or should I play it safe and buy a CD at my local bank?"

Of course, the prudent response on the part of your financial adviser would be to suggest some form of diversification; after all, he might say, you don't want to put all your eggs in one basket. Depending on your risk tolerance, long-term goals, and financial position, you should probably split the money into various piles and certainly not re-strict yourself to the all-or-nothing bank deposit or stock market choice.

But let's examine the all-or-nothing question in greater detail, fo-cusing on the two extreme alternatives. If you "take the plunge" and invest the $10,000 in the stock market, what are the odds that you will regret this decision? What is the probability that the stock market is the wrong place to invest your money?

In a sense, you may have noticed, those questions are really point-less. They are pointless because no meaningful answer can be deter-mined unless we specify an appropriate investment holding period. If you take the plunge, will you regret the decision tomorrow? Will you regret the decision in one year? Will you regret the decision in 10 years? When do you need the money?

Figure 3.3 illustrates what I call the time-adjusted "probability of fi-nancial regret." Over a 1-year time horizon, it shows that there is a 35% chance that a diversified portfolio of U.S. equities will under-perform the 5% rate of return from the safe bank deposit. What about a 10-year horizon? In that case, the chart shows that a diversified portfolio of U.S. equities has just an 11% probability of shortfall. In other words, there's a better than four-in-five chance that, over the next decade, the U.S. stock market will experience a rate of return that is greater than the re-turn currently available from a secure 5% bank deposit.

Finally, what if your time horizon is 35 years away? In this case, the chart indicates a probability of financial regret of roughly 1%. As the time horizon increases, the probability of shortfall decreases rap-idly; scientists like to say that it decays exponentially. It never actually hits zero—there are no guarantees in life—but it gets very close to zero. Time and financial risk are intricately intertwined.

Just as we must know the appropriate unit of time to comprehend a given speed, financial risk has an embedded dimension of time. Talk-ing about whether something is risky or safe without addressing the relevant time horizon and the financial alternatives is meaningless. In-deed, over a 1-year horizon, the stock market is clearly quite risky—relative to the secure alternative of putting the money in a CD. That's because the probability of shortfall, or regret from investing in stocks, is 35%.

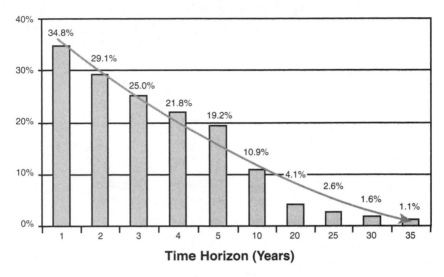

Probability of Regret

Broad Portfolio of U.S. Equities versus 5% Benchmark

Time Horizon (Years)

Figure 3.3   Patience is a financial virtue.

Source: Moshe Milevsky and the IFID Centre, 2008.

On the other hand, if you adopt a 35-year horizon, the stock market is quite safe, relative to the CD alternative. That's because the probability of regret would then be about 1%. The flip side of this implies a strong probability of success, of having made the right choice. That probability is close to 99%.

In fact, I would argue that over a 35-year horizon, the certificate of deposit, or the money market fund, for that matter, is the risky asset class, and the equity mutual fund is the safe asset class, especially when you look at it on an after-tax basis. But the larger point I'm trying to make is that you should examine the odds that are attached to various courses of action.

Should I Take More Risk When I'm Younger?

If you're wondering whether to take more risk when you're younger, the short answer is not necessarily, "It depends among other things on your human capital." Now for the long answer. To recap, investing is all about taking advantage of probabilities. If in any given year in the future there is a 50% chance that the stock market will decline, then the odds of getting two bear-market years in a row is 25%, 12.5% for three years, and so on. See Table 3.3 for the number out to seven years.

TABLE 3.3 Investing Is All About Probabilities

The Event (Duration of Bear Market)	Probability Hypothetical example
1 year	$(1/2)^1 = 50\%$
2 years	$(1/2)^2 = 25\%$
3 years	$(1/2)^3 = 12.5\%$
4 years	$(1/2)^4 = 6.25\%$
7 years	$(1/2)^7 = 0.78\%$

Source: Moshe Milevsky and the IFID Centre, 2008.

In discussing the concept of investment diversification, I have up to this point excluded potentially the greatest asset on your balance sheet—your human capital. While conceptually this asset is different from your tangible financial assets, it should actually be considered and diversified in tandem with your financial capital. This might sound like an abstract concept, but I will try to convince you that you can and should implement it as part of your risk management strategy over your life cycle. This is where the question, "Are you a stock or a bond?" comes in. By this I mean does your human capital exhibit the characteristics of a risky equity investment? For example, do you work in an investment banking firm where your compensation is somehow linked with the performance of an index such as the SP500? Or is your income more steady and predictable like a long-term government bond? For example, as a tenured university professor, I can say with confidence that I am a bond.

After you have analyzed the riskiness of your human capital, you should be using financial and investment capital to hedge it from potential losses; the same diversification principles that I discussed earlier are applicable.

Review the form of compensation that you receive in your place of work. For example, if you find that a significant portion of your compensation is received in the form of company stocks and options, then your total capital may be poorly diversified because the bulk of your human capital already rests with your place of work. Instead, and according to the main idea of diversification that I mentioned earlier, your invested assets should zig when your salary zags. If you find yourself in the situation in which your human capital and financial capital are zigging and zagging together, change the composition of one of them! Change your asset allocation, tilt your financial portfolio away from your human capital. Get compensated differently and revisit the structure of your 401k.

Alternatively in the other direction, your human capital can be viewed as a hedge against losses in your financial capital. Remember that over time, the probability that your diversified stock portfolio will earn less than a risk-free money market fund or bank account will decline. However, as you saw from the figures and tables, over a 30-year horizon there is still a chance you will do worse. However, and this is one of the key messages from this chapter, even if markets do not perform as well as expected and even if returns are not as good as in the past, you always have the option to continue working, save more, and perhaps cut down on your spending and expenses. Sure, this is not an ideal to aim for or something to aspire to, but let's be honest here. It is an option. This itself is valuable and can be used as a hedge against investment risk. Remember, after you are retired and moving toward the end of the life cycle, this option is not readily available and can't be relied upon to smooth out the investment bumps in the market. But in the accumulation or saving-for-retirement phase, it is definitely a reliable crutch.

So, as a 50-, 40-, or especially 30-year-old, you should be willing to take more chances with your total portfolio, perhaps even borrow to invest or leverage into the stock market, because you have the ability to mine more human capital if needed. Practically speaking, if your career and investments work out well, you can retire (or reduce your work load) at the age of 65. However, if you happen to get unlucky, you can delay your retirement by a few years and make up the lost market returns with more human capital. Again, this is not an ideal situation and not something you want to aim for in advance, but it's a fall-back strategy that also diversifies your total portfolio.

Summary

- Diversification is very important at all stages in life. This implies, among other things, that you should not allocate more than a small fraction of your 401(k) tax-deferred savings plan to company stock. You should make sure to have exposure to international stocks and alternative asset classes as well.

- Remember that the most valuable asset on your personal balance sheet is your human capital, which has characteristics of a stock or bond. The riskier your human capital, for example, the more it resembles a stock, the less stocks you should have in your investment portfolio and financial capital; inversely, the less risky, the more it resembles a bond.

- Over long time horizons, the probabilities favor investing in stocks/equities. This does not mean the risk disappears or goes away. It simply means that you have better odds.

- The real reason you can afford to take more diversified investment risk within your 401(k), when you are saving for retirement, is that you have an investment in human capital, which may behave more like a bond than a stock. You also have the option to delay retirement, which gives you a buffer against market risk and volatility.

Endnotes

An interesting and accessible paper by Jagannathan and Kocherlakota (1996) reviews the reasons why time and age might, or might not, play a role in the optimal asset allocation. One of the early works on the concept of time diversification is the monograph by Reichenstein and Dorsett (1995). The book by Siegel (2002) is by now a classic in the field, advocating that long-term investors should allocate a much larger percentage of their wealth to stocks, while the book by Bodie and Clowes (2003) takes the opposing view that investors are taking on too much risk and should allocate more toward fixed income bonds. For those who want to read up on the state of the art when it comes to asset allocation models, please refer to Campbell and Viceira (2002). In most of the book, I use the term "expected return" to denote the arithmetic mean. The arithmetic mean (AM) return is greater than the expected growth rate, aka the geometric mean (GM) return. To convert AM into GM, subtract half the volatility squared. For example, if AM = 7% and volatility is 20%, the GM = $0.07-(0.5)(0.2)^2 = 5\%$.

4

Debt Can Be Good at All Ages

"…I want to pay off all my loans in the next ten years, so that by the time I am retired I don't owe money, and I certainly want to make sure I don't die with any debt…."

Myth #4

As an undergraduate college student living and enjoying the '80s life in New York City, I amassed a fairly large amount of debt, accumulating a diversified portfolio of small loans owed to personal friends of mine and even my roommate. Although the liberal arts college I was attending had arranged for student loans and I had a part-time job boxing cartons in a bookstore, I didn't have any money left over at the end of the month. Looking around for a "solution" to my growing problem, I decided to apply for a credit card from one of the many companies flooding the campus with pamphlets. At the time, this seemed like the equivalent of "free money" to me because I still had not mastered the idea that a line of credit is not an asset, and that paying 25% interest might not be the greatest investment. Anyway, I eagerly sat down to fill in the paperwork for the credit card and got to the line in the application form where it said, "Cosigner must complete this section." That's when it hit me that this might not be as easy as it first sounded. So, I decided to approach my grandfather to be a cosigner, because I presumed that they were looking for somebody "old and wise" to vouch for my good character. He had just retired as a high school principal in Cleveland. So, I broached the topic with him one day when I was visiting. Not wanting to get too complicated, I asked him vaguely if he could help out and sign some paperwork I needed from the bank. He took a brief look at the credit card application, and then proceeded to give me a 45-minute sermon about the evils of debt, credit cards, and living beyond one's means. He actually went on to quote Shakespeare's *Hamlet*, "Neither a borrower nor a lender be, for loan oft loses both itself and friend, and borrowing dulls the edge of husbandry..." Basically, he hated debt and I had no cosigner. End of story.

As I later learned, my grandfather had experienced and still vividly remembered the calamitous events of 1929 and the ensuing economic depression that followed. In fact, the only time I heard him preach more fervently against a financial instrument, was when I asked him whether he had any money in the stock market. (If you can't guess, he didn't.)

As I discussed in Chapter 1, "You, Inc.," almost two-thirds of U.S. households have some form of debt on their personal balance sheet. It is hard to know how much of this debt has been incurred for good reasons, such as buying a house, starting a business, or getting a graduate degree, and how much debt is accumulating for the wrong reasons. Either way, the main message of this chapter is that debt that is properly utilized and managed can be a very effective component of your comprehensive financial strategy. The main problem with debt occurs when you are paying very high interest rates or using the funds to acquire assets that pay no dividends. But, borrowing money to invest in assets that are expected (although not guaranteed) to earn more than the interest rate you are paying on your loan, can be an excellent idea at all stages of the life cycle. The notion of using other people's (the bank's) money to invest, also known as leverage, is quite alluring and extremely lucrative. Indeed, you would recognize many of the names, such as Donald Trump, who can attribute a large part of their success to the concept of leverage. And so, with all due respect to my grandfather, I believe that careful, judicious leveraging is a sure way to grow wealth, although it does have its risks.

In this chapter, I provide an in-depth analysis of the mechanics of borrowing money for the purposes of investing, whether it be in a personal residence, general real estate, or even the stock market. My overall objective is to illustrate how the concept and existence of human capital relates to debt management and the optimal investment portfolio. At the end of the chapter, I provide some indication of how much debt is prudent at various stages of the human life cycle.

The Good, the Bad, and the Ugly of Leverage

Leverage, once again, in this context at least, simply means borrowing money to invest. The great stock market returns experienced in recent years have tempted many investors into precisely that risky proposition.

Now, you might be thinking that you don't engage in this risky strategy and this chapter likely doesn't apply to you at all. In reality, however, leverage isn't necessarily risky or rare. It is more common than you might think, and you might even unknowingly be engaging in the strategy yourself. What do I mean by this? As you can see from Table 4.1, most people who live in and (partially) own their house have a mortgage, which means they are leveraged. In fact, if you buy a house with 10% money down, and hence you borrow 90%, your debt to equity ratio is 9-to-1. This is on par with some hedge funds! So, you just might not be as immune from the risks of leverage as you thought. At the very least, you should spend a bit of time examining and thinking about You, Inc.'s debt-to-equity ratio as well as the optimal capital structure, which is another way of saying the balance between debt and equity.

TABLE 4.1 Does Your Family Unit Own a House?

Age	% Owning a House	Median Value°	Mortgage on Residence°
Total	69.1	$160,000	47.9%
Under 35	41.6	$135,000	37.7%
35 to 44	68.3	$160,000	62.8%
45 to 54	77.3	$170,000	64.6%
55 to 64	79.1	$200,000	51.0%
65 to 74	81.3	$150,000	32.1%
75 or older	85.2	$125,000	18.7%

*For those who owned their principal residence

Data Source: U.S. Federal Reserve Consumer Finances Survey 2004, Table 11 04.

The basic arithmetic of leverage is simple and compelling. Suppose you have $10,000 invested in a mutual fund and the mutual fund goes up by 15% in one year. That means you've made $1,500 on your original $10,000 investment. Now, that's nice, but it could be a lot nicer. This is because if you could somehow borrow an additional $10,000 (the equivalent of 100% leverage) and invest $20,000 ($10,000 + $10,000) in the mutual fund, you will have made a lot more by year's end.

With a 15% return, the $20,000 would become $23,000. Of course, from that amount you would have to subtract the original loan of $10,000, plus any interest that you might have paid—say, $500 (5% on $10,000). That would leave you with $12,500. Wow! You started with $10,000 and turned it into $12,500, a full $1,000 more than if you had not borrowed. That's the equivalent of a 25% return. In other words, you've leveraged the fund's 15% return into a 25% return. That's what I call "the good."

Given the potential power of leverage, it's no wonder that investors, back in 1998, were rushing out to remortgage their homes, cottages, boats, and children to invest the proceeds in the stock market. As long as (after-tax) interest payments were lower than your investment earnings, you would end up ahead of the game. In fact, if you borrowed $20,000 for every $10,000 you owned—a leverage factor of 200%—you could have earned 35% on your original $10,000. The only constraint might have been a financial institution that placed restrictions on leverage or margining ratios—or perhaps a financial planner with some common sense. For example, some brokerages might restrict the amount you can borrow to 50% or perhaps 80% of the value of your investments. So, if you have $100,000 in stocks, you can buy another $50,000 to $80,000 on margin. This way you would have, say, $180,000 in assets, $80,000 in debt, and the same $100,000 in personal equity.

The arithmetic works in reverse as well. Yes, if markets move up by 15% a year, everything is peachy keen. But if markets suddenly drop 25% in one year (or worse, in one quarter), then you not only lose 25% on your original investment of $10,000, you lose 25% on the borrowed money as well. When it comes time to pay back the loan, the problems start to pile up.

For example, if you had borrowed $10,000—for total assets of $20,000—then a 25% loss wipes out $5,000 of your capital, leaving you with $15,000 at the end of the year. To add insult to injury, you must pay back the $10,000 loan, plus the (assumed) 5% interest. At year's end, therefore, your equity (your assets minus your liabilities) has dwindled to a mere $4,500. Your original equity investment of $10,000 has lost 55% of its value, even though the market (fund, stock) only fell 25%. That's "the ugly" side of leverage.

So, should you leverage? Is it a good idea? Will you make money? After all, in the long run, markets go up, don't they? Well, by now you should know that there are no simple answers to these questions; all you can do is look at the odds. What are the odds that you will benefit from leverage? What are the odds that you will regret exercising it? First, let's take a good look at the upside. Suppose you are faced with a stock, mutual fund, or investment that is expected to earn 15% on average, in the long run. However, because there are no free lunches in the world, you have to contend with some risk. Assume that the volatility risk of this particular investment is 30%. So, facing this kind of investment, what happens if you leverage yourself?

You must pay particular attention to two factors: the leverage ratio and the borrowing (margin account) interest rate. Both will affect your outcome and the odds. The leverage ratio is the amount that you borrow to invest, expressed as a percentage of your original equity or capital. For example, if you have $10,000 and borrow $10,000, your leverage ratio is 100%. If you borrow only $5,000, your leverage ratio is 50%. If you don't borrow at all, your leverage ratio is 0%.

Next is the interest rate factor. This is simply the after-tax rate of interest that you'll be paying on the borrowed capital. In the present climate, the rate can range anywhere from 3% to 10%, depending on many considerations. The most important of these are your credit worthiness and the odds of your going bankrupt. Clearly, you want to borrow at the lowest possible interest rate so that you get to keep as much of your market gains as possible.

When you put the two factors together—leverage ratio and interest costs—you can do some intelligent analysis of how the leverage will affect your investments. The numbers in Tables 4.2 through 4.4 come from a Monte Carlo computer simulation. Monte Carlo computer simulations generate millions of different scenarios that estimate the probabilities of earning various return levels, both with and without leverage. The tables that follow report the probabilities for a variety of outcomes.

TABLE 4.2   Leverage: The Good—What Are the Chances of Doubling the Market? (Market Expected Return: 15%; Volatility: 30%)

Leverage Ratio	Interest Cost		
	3%	5%	7%
0%	30.9%	30.9%	30.9%
25%	37.4%	36.9%	36.4%
50%	42.1%	41.2%	40.3%
100%	48.0%	46.7%	45.4%
250%	55.7%	53.8%	51.9%

Source: Moshe Milevsky and the IFID Centre, 2008.

Here's how to read Table 4.2. Assume that you are paying 5% interest on your margin account. If you leverage at a rate of 100%—one borrowed dollar for every dollar of original equity investment capital —then the odds of earning double the market rate (that is, $2 \times 15\%$ = 30%) on your investment are 46.7%. In other words, the chances of converting $10,000 into $13,000 are 46.7%. That's slightly less than a one-in-two chance of doubling the market.

Compare that to the chances of earning the same 30% ($2 \times 15\%$) if you don't leverage at all. Then, as Table 4.2 illustrates, your zero-leverage chances are a mere 30.9%. This is less than one chance in three. Notice the huge increase in the probability of doing very well if you leverage. Sound tempting? Many have been lured.

Of course, as you can see from Table 4.2, if you have to pay more than 5% on your margin account, the odds of doing better than doubling the market will go down a bit. That's simply because the market has to earn even more, which is even less likely, to pay back your higher-interest borrowing. Likewise, if your interest cost is lower than 5%, your odds are somewhat better, but not by much. The real improvement in odds comes from higher amounts of leverage.

Look at the 250% leverage ratio case. Now, for the same doubling-the-market result, at a 5% margin, the numbers increase to 53.8%. This is a 53.8% chance (better than one in two) that you will earn more than a 30% return on your original investment. In fact, the higher your leverage ratio, the better your odds up to a point. It's not surprising that so many have rushed to leverage their capital: The odds look so good.

Now, however, let's examine "the bad," the downside. What are the odds that you will lose money? What are the odds that, with leverage, you will end up with less than when you started?

Table 4.3 shows what happens when things go wrong. Although the odds of doubling the market are much greater for the leverage case, the odds of losing money are higher as well. For example, if you leverage yourself at 100% with a margin cost of 5%, the odds of losing money—that is, the chances of having less than your original equity capital at year's end—are 33.8%.

TABLE 4.3   Leverage: The Bad—What Are the Chances of Losing Money? (Market Expected Return: 15%; Volatility: 30%)

	Interest Cost		
Leverage Ratio	3%	5%	7%
0%	30.9%	30.9%	30.9%
25%	31.6%	32.0%	32.5%
50%	32.0%	32.8%	33.6%
100%	32.6%	33.8%	35.1%
250%	33.4%	35.2%	36.9%

Source: Moshe Milevsky and the IFID Centre, 2008.

Thus, if you start with $10,000 and borrow $10,000, at year's end, after paying back your loan with interest, the probability of having less than $10,000 is 33.8%.

"Wait a minute," you might say. As you can see, 33.8% is not that much higher than the 30.9% chance of losing money if you don't use leverage at all. In other words, there's only a 3% greater chance that using leverage will court disaster. That doesn't sound so bad, does it? Is that the sum total of your risk? Well, not exactly. Here's "the ugly."

To give you an indication of how ugly things can get with leverage, Table 4.4 provides the probability of losing a quarter of your initial investment from a leveraged transaction. The question is, "What are the odds that if you start off with $10,000 and borrow, you'll be left with less than $7,500 after 12 months?" This would be a 25% loss of equity capital.

TABLE 4.4   Leverage: The Ugly—What Are the Chances of Losing a Quarter of Your Initial Investment? (Market Expected Return: 15%; Volatility: 30%)

	Interest Cost		
Leverage Ratio	**3%**	**5%**	**7%**
0%	9.1%	9.1%	9.1%
25%	12.6%	12.9%	13.1%
50%	15.3%	15.9%	16.4%
100%	19.3%	20.2%	21.2%
250%	25.2%	26.8%	28.4%

Source: Moshe Milevsky and the IFID Centre, 2008.

If you don't leverage at all, the chances of suffering such a drastic reduction of capital are about 9%. But if you choose the 100% leverage route, and you pay a margin interest cost of 5%, the odds of losing a quarter of your initial investment are close to 20%. That's a one-in-five chance. Why are the odds so high? After all, the odds of doing very well were quite high as well. How can the odds be so high for both the good and the ugly?

Well, that's the key point with investment leverage. You are subjecting yourself to extremes. Things can go very well—or very badly. Very well if the market goes up; very badly if the market goes down. I like to say that leverage exaggerates both the severe upside and the severe downside.

On a technical level, you have increased the potential return of your investment, but you have increased the uncertainty as well. The higher uncertainty means that you are more likely to experience the extreme cases. In the good times, the extremes will be welcome. In the bad, they can bring you to the brink of bankruptcy.

Of course, it's unfortunate that you must take the bad (downside risk) with the good (upside potential). But that's precisely why most investment houses and federal regulators prohibit large amounts of leverage at the individual investor level, and justifiably. There is however, one way to eliminate, or at least greatly reduce, the chances of a wretched outcome. That is, buy a product with upside potential, but that can't lose money. Sound impossible? Well, investments with money-back guarantees, such as index-linked notes and put-protected portfolios, are all products where the "left tail" is eliminated. The names might sound odd and confusing, but the main idea is the same. By "left tail," I mean those events where your final wealth is less than your initial wealth.

These crash-proof investments, in all their guises, promise to return your original principal in the event of a bear market, or worse, at the expense of marginally lower returns. This essentially guarantees that you will have enough money to pay back the outstanding loan at its maturity.

Of course, there is no guarantee that the return on these products will beat the interest costs that you must pay on your borrowings, but at least the chance of a true catastrophe is eliminated. In sum, the most important thing to remember when contemplating leverage is that you must be able to afford the interest payments, without having to sell out at the worst possible time.

Is Debt Good?

In this chapter, I looked at whether using leverage—"borrowing to invest" in the purest sense—is a prudent strategy. First, if your interest cost is tax-deductible, and market returns are treated as capital gains, which means taxes are deferred as long as you don't sell, then the upside of leverage can look quite appealing. By the same token, the downside is obvious. If things go wrong, and they certainly can, your loss is magnified. As Table 4.4 demonstrated, the odds of suffering a severe loss of your original equity are quite high.

Putting It All Together

I have now come to a critical juncture in this book, where I can finally bring together my thoughts on the benefits of debt and leverage, together with the role of human capital and the main thesis regarding You, Inc. as a stock or a bond. It is now time to analyze the complete portfolio choice: investments, careers, and insurance, over the entire life cycle.

Let's start with a 45-year-old investment banker who earns $100,000 per year; he has a stay-at-home wife raising his dependent young children at home. By virtue of his job in the financial services industry, with compensation that is very much contingent on the vagaries of the stock market, his human capital is definitely a stock—at least for the most part. Let's further make life and numbers easier by assuming he has $250,000 in a 401(k) or IRA, or similar long-term investment account. Let's ignore housing for now. According to a model I developed and published with various colleagues at the IFID Centre (the results of which are displayed in Table 4.5) he should allocate 60% of his retirement savings account (that is, $150,000 of $250,000) to equity investments that are highly correlated with the stock market. The other 40% (or $100,000 of the $250,000 retirement account) should be allocated to bonds and safer fixed income instruments. As I have argued before, this is because he is already endowed with a very high exposure to stocks within his human capital. This is not a speculative decision or bearish bet on the direction of the stock market, rather (as I have stressed many times before) it is a hedge for his human capital.

In contrast, a tenured professor who earns the same $100,000 per year, with the same number of dependents and personal family situation, can afford to allocate or invest 280% of her nest egg in the risky stock market. The 280% implies that she should allocate a full 100% of the same $250,000-sized retirement savings account. She should then borrow (leverage, buy on margin) another 180% worth of stock. In other words she should actually borrow $450,000 and invest that in the stock market as well, for a total portfolio asset value of $700,000. This method might seem outrageous and imprudent at first glance—and especially for a conservative professor, no less—but it strikes at the heart of the "human capital is stock versus bond" thesis. The tenured professor is sitting on millions of dollars worth of implicit bonds. Without engaging in the leverage transaction, her personal balance sheet would contain a skewed and unhealthy allocation to bonds. Therefore, to bring her personal equity into balance, she should borrow money—effectively shorting bonds and neutralizing some of her holdings—and invest the proceeds in stocks. She is not speculating, gambling, or imprudently squandering her hard-earned money. Rather, once again, she is hedging. She is making sure that her total balance sheet and not just her financial balance sheet is diversified.

TABLE 4.5   Investment Debt, Life Insurance, and Equity Holdings: The Impact of Being a Stock Versus Bond

		You earn $100,000 per year			
		Tenured Professor	**Bankruptcy Lawyer**	**Mechanical Engineer**	**Investment Banker**
Age 45	Equity Allocation	280%*	170%*	125%*	60%
	Life Insurance	$1.9m	$1.5m	$1.4m	$1.3m
Age 55	Equity Allocation	85%	70%	50%	35%
	Life Insurance	$0.8m	$0.6m	$0.5m	$0.4m

*Equity allocations above 100% indicate leverage; that is, borrowing money to invest in risky equity.

Source: The IFID Centre; model developed by H. Huang and M. Milevsky.

The life insurance perspective, which is the second part of the table, tells a similar story. The investment banker with a superficially identical financial situation as the tenured professor should hold much less life insurance because the economic value of his human capital is riskier and hence lower. I repeat, he might be expecting to earn the same $100,000 per year going forward compared to the tenured professor, but given the risky nature of the income and salary, only a fraction must be insured. Once again it all boils down to the protection and diversification element. Life insurance is not speculation or gambling on death. It is a hedge against the sudden demise of human capital. The discounted economic value of an income stream is greatest when the cashflows are stable and predictable. And, while both the professor and the banker might be expecting to earn the same $100,000 per year, the variability or volatility of the banker's wages are much higher. Hence, the present discounted value is less. Hence, he buys less insurance.

In contrast to the two extremes, the mechanical engineer, whose human capital dynamics are not necessarily correlated with the stock market at all will be counseled to own more stocks compared to the investment banker, although not as much stock as the tenured professor. Likewise, the corporate bankruptcy specialist, whose fortunes and success are greater in times of corporate sector financial stress, is counseled within this model to take more equity exposure. They all at 45 years of age earn the same income, have the same financial assets on the balance sheet, and the same financial obligations at home, yet their portfolio looks completely different. Why? Some people are stocks, some people are bonds, and everyone else is a combination in between.

Now let me examine the impact of aging, ten years later, on this "stock or bond" thesis. Let's revisit the investment banker ten years later, at the age of 55. Abstracting from any personal circumstances and assuming he has managed to accumulate the same amount of financial capital as the tenured professor, his optimal equity exposure now drops from 60% of his retirement account at the age of 45, to 35% of the retirement account at the age of 55. The reason he should have even less equity exposure now is because he is aging, has less time until retirement, and simply can't afford the risk. The impact of time on shortfall risk, which I elaborated on in the previous chapter, also acts to reduce the optimal equity exposure. The tenured professor also reduces her equity exposure with age, but she still has 85% in the stock market.

The mechanical engineer and the bankruptcy lawyer are once again counseled to hold lower levels of risky equity compared to the professor, but greater amounts compared to the banker. The optimal amount of life insurance is also somewhere in between. Of course, this story abstracts from the rather obvious fact that an investment banker is likely to accumulate much more financial wealth by age 55, compared to a mechanical engineer or professor. These numbers live in an artificial world that economists call *ceteris paribus*, which means, "all else being equal."

If I were to expand this table for yet another 10 or 15 years, well into the retirement of the professor and banker, you would see that the optimal amount of life insurance would get close to zero and their investment portfolios would look rather similar. I get into this story in the next few chapters, but after the human capital has been converted to financial capital, there is very little income left to hedge.

Either way, despite the highly idealized and very abstract nature of the preceding story and the numbers contained in Table 4.5, there are some reliable and robust qualitative takeaways that remain true regardless of the actual parameters and careers. These further reinforce some of the ideas I discussed in earlier chapters.

First of all, the age-old general rule that you should allocate your numerical age value to bonds—or 100 minus your age value to stocks—is somewhat meaningless at best, and wrong at worst. Even if you revise the number from 100 to 110 or even 120 it certainly doesn't capture the essence or risk classification of your job. For some occupations and time points in your life the optimal allocation to equities might be greater than 100 minus age, and in other cases it might be lower. Your age value doesn't contain enough information to determine a suitable asset allocation.

Likewise, borrowing money is traditionally viewed negatively. On a personal note, I know that it's deeply frowned upon by individuals from a certain older generation. Yet, in this chapter I have argued that debt cannot be examined in isolation. Rather, it is a component of a bigger issue, which is the optimal total capital structure for You, Inc. When analyzed properly, it's just another dimension of the asset allocation dilemma. For many individuals whose human capital and jobs are safe or reliable, there is a very strong argument to be made for having much more than 100% of your nest egg invested in the stock market. I myself practice what I preach and am leveraged to the tune of about 2-to-1. Indeed, I can attest that today this can easily be done with investment loans and margin accounts where the interest rate is quite reasonable.

Counterintuitively, the most conservative of professions—the government employee or the tenured professor—which attract the most risk averse among us, are ideally the investors who should be taking on the greatest amount of investment risk, if only they looked at their entire personal balance sheet as opposed to just their liquid investment account.

In the next few chapters I continue the journey over the life cycle and discuss what happens when you have spent your human capital (that is, you are in retirement) and it's time to figure out how to allocate your financial capital. At that stage, your previous job classification is not as relevant as your pension entitlement and the security of your guaranteed sources of income. But first, let's talk about what things might cost in the future. The next chapter takes a look at inflation.

Summary

- There is nothing evil or wrong with debt. It is just another financial strategy. Moreover, debt for investment purposes makes perfect sense. Just ensure that the interest you are paying on your debt is less (on average) than the return you are earning on the borrowed funds.

- One of the implications of this chapter is that dying with debt might not be as odious as it sounds, as long as the personal equity on your balance sheet is positive. In other words, if your house is worth $500,000 and you owe $200,000, then your personal equity is positive. Net worth is what matters.

- When you borrow money to invest, you are increasing the chances of financial shocks. Make sure you can withstand these shocks and have the funds to cover the interest payments during turbulent times.

- Finally, if your human capital is more bond-like, for example, if you have a secure job with a predictable income stream, you might be overexposed to bonds and hence might be able to afford to borrow money to invest, even if you don't need the loan. In fact, the best loans are exactly the ones you don't need.

Endnotes

Clearly, the topics of debt, mortgages, and prudent leverage have been in the news lately, and one cannot overemphasize the extent to which this issue is intertwined with personal housing. The article by Goetzmann (1993) provides an accessible approach to treating real estate and one's home as part of the asset allocation decision. The book by Evensky and Katz (2006) contains a collection of articles, many of which deal with issues relating to debt and borrowing as part of the personal capital structure.

5

Personal Inflation and the Retirement Cost of Living

"...Inflation is much lower than it has been in the past because the central bank is doing a great job, so I don't have to worry about this too much...."

Myth #5

Growing up in Latin America during the 1980s, I quickly learned how to adapt to the impact of inflation in daily life. With annual inflation rates reaching over triple digits, even young children knew to never expect the same price twice. Cash wasn't allowed to sit idle and interest rates on bank deposits were designed to outpace inflation. We knew that salaries were linked to the U.S. dollar and pension income was stated in *unidades reales*, which is effectively a pseudo-currency consisting of a basket of consumable goods. Yes, complicated, but a fact of life.

Then, as I moved back to a monetarily stable North American environment, the debilitating power of inflation moved to my mental back burner. It toppled down my list of risks and worries. After all, the consumer price index (CPI) in the U.S. has increased by an average compound rate of only 2.96% per annum over the last quarter century of available data. Indeed, 25 years ago I was just starting high school and 2.96% was considered a decent weekly rate of inflation in many parts of the world. So clearly, the U.S. has been quite fortunate and blessed with low inflation rates. Table 5.1 lists the somewhat varied, yet relatively low average rates of inflation for recent decades. It is easy to get lulled into a false sense of security that inflation is just not an issue anymore. The Federal Reserve's main policy mandate is to keep prices stable and even a whiff of unexpected pressure sends them into a tightening tizzy.

TABLE 5.1   Average Annual Inflation in the U.S.

Decade...	Rate...
1950s	2.1%
1960s	2.8%
1970s	7.9%
1980s	4.7%
1990s	2.8%

Data Source: CPI-U index, Bureau of Labor Statistics; IFID Centre calculations.

In this chapter, I take a much closer and more careful look at inflation and show you how it actually varies depending on your age and how, exactly, it is impacted by the way you spend your money. Oddly enough, you create your own inflation, and I'll explain what that means. When you are young, earning a salary and, therefore, in the process of converting human capital into financial capital, your equity-based investments tend to keep up with inflation. In all likelihood wages grow at a positive real (after inflation) rate over time, so that inflation is just not that much of a threat in your working years. If inflation picks up, you will likely demand a raise or bonus from your employer to keep up with the cost of living. Inflation is not high on the list of financial enemies during your working years.

But in the area of retirement income planning, things are very different. I believe that the relatively low inflation rates we have experienced in the last quarter century might actually be just as dangerous as the hyperinflation rates I grew up with in Latin America. This is because low numbers can be easily ignored. Yet, over long horizons they can be just as deadly, especially if you are not compensated for this risk and don't know your own inflation rate. Once again, one of the main financial risks we face as we age is our unknown and age-specific personal inflation rate. It is at retirement that management of inflation risk is especially important because you tend to have the most finan-cial capital at stake and might no longer have your human capital to mine.

Back to Basics: Inflation's Impact

Table 5.2 illustrates the impact of relatively benign inflation rates over long periods of time. Here is how to read this table: Imagine you are getting a $1,000 pension income check every single month of your retirement years, but that this check is not adjusted for inflation. What this means is that your nominal income stays at $1,000, but its real pur-chasing power declines steadily with time. As you age, the same check buys you less. The table tells exactly how much $1,000 will buy you in today's dollars, depending on the value of inflation going forward.

TABLE 5.2   Inflation: What Does a $1,000 Payment Really Buy You?

Year #	0%	1%	2%	4%
1	$1,000	$905	$820	$676
15	$1,000	$861	$743	$555
20	$1,000	$820	$673	$456
25	$1,000	$780	$610	$375
30	$1,000	$742	$552	$308
35	$1,000	$706	$500	$253

Source: Moshe Milevsky and the IFID Centre, 2008.

Notice that increasing the inflation rate from 2% to 4% per year can erode the purchasing power of $1,000 by almost 40%, from $610 to $375, at the 25-year horizon. I picked 25 years because it is the me-dian remaining lifespan for a newly retired couple, and a 2% to 4% in-flation rate is arguably a reasonable aggregate range. During 2007, inflation in the U.S. hit the level of 4%.

Actually, the inflation story gets even more interesting. It seems the U.S. Department of Labor (DoL), via their Bureau of Labor Sta-tistics (BLS) has created an entirely new experimental inflation index for the elderly. They called it the CPI-E and it is meant to better capture the inflation rate that is unique for Americans age 62 and older, the group that comprises roughly 17 percent of the U.S. population (see Figure 5.1).

Source: Financial Times, May 14, 2007

Figure 5.1   CPI isn't perfect, accurate, or relevant...to you.

Why would inflation be different for the elderly? In fact, how does inflation get measured, at all? Let me back up a bit. The answer to these questions comes down to our spending habits. Boiled down to its essence, statisticians measure inflation partially based on how we spend our money.

Basically, they measure price changes for hundreds of categories and items each month. Some of these items increase in price while others decline or stay the same. The weights placed on the different categories and items reflect our average spending habits. If the typical American spends three times more money on banana products than avocado products, then the index weight placed on bananas is three times as high as the index weight placed on avocados. This is regardless of whether you personally are allergic to bananas and love avocados.

The consumer price index for wage earners and clerical workers is labeled and abbreviated CPI-W. The letter W is meant to remind us that this is the inflation rate experienced by wage earners. This index reflects the spending habits of this group, which is about 32% of the U.S. population. As of mid-2007, working Americans spend about four times the amount on food and beverages than on apparel, and they spend eight times more on housing-related expenditures than they do on recreation, and so on. These weights do change over time, but the relative values are fairly stable. The components in Table 5.3 provide the weights on the various categories that make up the CPI-W in mid-2007, and they, of course, must add up to 1. Notice that each subcategory has its own inflation rate. The higher the group weighting or relative importance, the more a price change for the group will impact the overall inflation rate.

TABLE 5.3   What's Your Inflation Rate?

Component	CPI-W		CPI-E	
	Relative Importance	*10-Year Inflation*	*Relative Importance*	*10-Year Inflation*
All items	1.00	26.5%	1.00	29.7%
Apparel	0.04	−8.3%	0.02	−8.8%
Education	0.06	18.2%	0.03	4.5%
Food and Beverage	0.16	25.9%	0.13	25.4%
Housing	0.40	32.8%	0.48	34.0%
Medical Care	0.05	47.8%	0.11	47.8%
Recreation	0.05	9.8%	0.05	18.3%
Transportation	0.20	20.4%	0.14	21.9%
Other	0.04	56.0%	0.04	45.5%

Data Source: Bureau of Labor Statistics data to end of 2006; IFID Centre calculations.

As you can see from Table 5.3, the relative importance placed on the various subcomponents differs for the regular (CPI-W) versus the new and experimental elderly (CPI-E) version. For example, in the CPI-E, Medical Care has twice the weight as it has in the CPI-W. The reason for this is because the elderly spend a greater fraction of their income on medical care. At the opposite end is the weighting that is placed on Food and Beverage. Its relative importance in the elderly inflation rate is 0.13 compared to 0.16 for the working rate. Table 5.4 shows the change in median expenditure over the entire U.S. population on these two items as we age. You can see that while in our forties and fifties, we spend almost three times more on food and beverage than on medical care. By the time we get into our late 70s, our food and beverage expenditure is only a fraction of our medical care expenses.

TABLE 5.4   Consumer Expenditure Survey:
U.S. Department of Labor (BLS) 2005

Annual Average	Age: 45–54	Age: 55–64	Age: 65–74	Age: 75+
Food & Beverage	$7,438	$6,656	$5,224	$3,555
Medical Care	$2,672	$3,410	$4,176	$4,210
Ratio of Food & Beverage to Medical Care	**2.78**	**1.95**	**1.25**	**0.84**

Source: Consumer Expenditures in 2005 (annual report), U.S. Department of Labor, Bureau of Labor Statistics.

I often see surprised reactions when people learn that a private room in a nursing home can cost as much as $330 per day, depending on the geographical location. Table 5.5 displays a sample average for this expense, which partially contributes to the rise in medical care costs that are seen in retirement. And while the topic of long-term care insurance—as well as general estate planning, Medicare, Medicaid, and other retirement risks—are well beyond the scope of this book, suffice it to say that one should give serious considerations to these issues. Health-related expenditures will become a much larger component of your spending and financial constraints as you age, which, among other things, means that inflation for medical care will have a greater impact on your personal inflation rate.

Here is the bottom line regarding retiree inflation as it pertains to retirement income planning. From early 1982 until late December 2006, the compound annual inflation rate in the U.S. as measured by the regular inflation rate for wage earners was 2.96% per annum.

During the exact same period, the inflation rate for the elderly was 3.30%, which is an average of almost 35 basis points per annum (or 0.35%) more over the last 25 years. This adds up to a difference of almost 15% over the 25-year period.

TABLE 5.5   Nursing Home Cost, Private Room

Location	Avg. Daily	Avg. Annual
San Francisco, CA	$371	$135,415
New York, NY	$352	$128,480
Boston, MA	$297	$108,405
Tulsa, OK	$163	$59,495
Wichita, KS	$157	$57,305
Baton Rouge, LA	$123	$44,895

Data Source: The MetLife Market Survey of Nursing Home & Assisted Living Costs, October 2007; IFID Centre calculations.

Now, my main point here is *not* that you should add another percentage point to your retirement income inflation projections. I don't think the CPI-E is relevant to you either, since it is also an average over a very large and diverse group of people. Rather, my main point is the fact that the Department of Labor bothers to compute an inflation rate for retirees should remind us that inflation is personal and unique. After all, if there is a CPI-E, why not a CPI-ME or a CPI-YOU? Depending on where you live, how you spend your money, how old you are, and even your gender, inflation is different.

Here is yet another example. The average inflation rate for the last ten years in Atlanta was 2.3%, compared to an average of 3.5% in San Diego. Likewise, a recent research report by Merrill Lynch quantifies the extent to which inflation is gender-based. According to their chief economist, the recent inflation rate for females has been about 3.6% and for males it is closer to 0.2%. Why? Their spending habits are different.

We all have slightly different and personal inflation rates based on spending habits. And as the owner of You, Inc., your task is to make sure that your newly invested financial capital keeps up with your very personal inflation rate, not some macro economic average. This is the true liability benchmark.

If you think about it for a moment, all else being equal, your human capital does a better job of keeping up with inflation compared to your financial capital. After all, salary and wages tend to be linked to inflation, albeit indirectly. However, once you are retired and have spent or converted most of your human capital into financial capital, inflation becomes a greater threat.

For those who are not yet convinced, Figure 5.2 provides yet another way to think about this and is a graphical illustration of the numbers in Table 5.3. As you can see, the elderly spend differently.

The Elderly Spend Differently:
Relative to Typical Wage-earner CPI

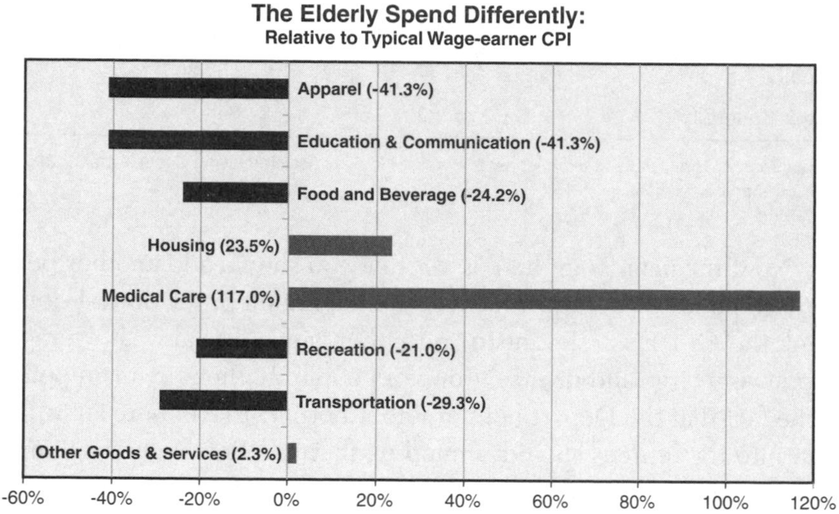

Figure 5.2   **Inflation is not an atmospheric phenomenon.**

Data Source: Bureau of Labor Statistics; IFID Centre calculations.

What is the practical side of all of this? First, sit down and conduct a very careful analysis of your expenditures and spending allocations. In fact, perhaps you might want to start by creating your rough inflation rate based on how you actually spend your money as well as where you live. Use the numbers and inflation rates in Table 5.3 to create a personal inflation rate, or do some extra homework and dig up the rate based on where you live.

Just as a very hypothetical example, imagine that your retirement spending consists of only two consumption goods: housing and medical care. You consume or spend money on these two categories in equal amounts. In this case your personal inflation over the last ten years would have been cumulative (34% + 48%)/2 = 41% and the annualized inflation rate would have been roughly $(1.41)^{(1/10)} - 1 = 3.5\%$ per year.

Note, once again, that the BLS doesn't calculate inflation by keeping these weights fixed for ten years—and they have a unique way of measuring house inflation—but you hopefully appreciate my basic point. Anyone can construct a rough personalized inflation rate that better reflects his expenditures.

Another important takeaway point is as follows: Because locating fixed-income investments that perfectly hedge your financial capital against a particular inflation rate is exceedingly difficult, the next best thing is to locate investments that have strong correlations with your liabilities.

For example, I would tilt my equity-based investment portfolio toward sectors and companies that stand to benefit from an (unpredictable) shock to my personal inflation rate. Companies in the pharmaceutical sector, biotechnology, health care, and even managers of nursing homes will all stand to benefit from further advances in longevity. If Pfizer, Merck, Wyeth, GlaxoSmithKline, or Bayer discover and develop a drug that extends my life by a handful of years, then my cost of longevity will obviously increase. More importantly, these companies' stock prices will likely increase above and beyond the underlying markets in which they trade. Investing in these companies will then hedge or even partially insure against the unexpected increase in retirement expenditures, which is yet another form of personal inflation.

Finally, one topic I have not addressed is whether the calculation methodology for CPI is a good measure of the economy's overall inflation rate. There are many financial commentators who believe that, irrespective of the personal nature of inflation, the true level of inflation in the economy is actually much higher, and that the reported numbers are lower than they should be. This is because the statistical methodology is biased by artificial values for many of the consumer prices that are hard to measure. Either way the end result is the same. It's time to pay more attention to this.

In sum, as you can see from Figure 5.3, inflation doesn't age well. Generic macro economic projections between 2% and 4% don't capture the personal nature of inflation for retirees. In my mind, CPI-ME is a unique risk-label for a very personal adversary that must be constantly battled.

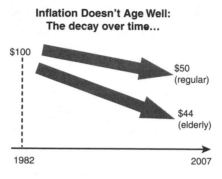

Figure 5.3   Things get even worse.

Source: Moshe Milevsky and the IFID Centre, 2008.

Summary

- True inflation is personal and not an atmospheric phenomenon. Learn to distinguish between your personal cost of living and the population inflation rate.

- The Consumer Price Index, which is the widely cited measure of inflation, is calculated as an average of an average and is meant to give a picture of the economy as a whole and not your personal experiences.

- As you age your inflation rate is likely higher, as measured by the newly created CPI-E for the elderly. The CPI-E has often exceeded the CPI since it has been calculated. Likely, this is because the elderly spend their money on goods and services that tend to appreciate at a higher rate over time.

- Make sure your investments and your retirement income keep up with your personal inflation rate. Although you might need less money during retirement—and that is debatable—I would assume that your required expenses and your personal inflation will increase by 5% to 8% per year.

Endnotes

See the book by Eisenberg (2006) and the collection of articles by Evensky and Katz (2006) for additional information on the "cost of living" for retirees. Visit the Bureau of Labor Statistics (BLS) website, www.bls.gov, to learn more about the components of the Consumer Price Index (CPI) as well as the CPI-E for the elderly. Alternatively, spend some time reading the recent speeches and testimony of Professor Ben Bernake, who is the chairman of the U.S. Federal Reserve and one of the world's leading scholars on the topic.

6

Sequence of Investment Returns

"...The mutual fund I own earned 9% during the last ten years, so I am obviously much better off than my neighbor whose fund only earned 8% over the same period...."

Myth #6

The ancient biblical story of Joseph and Pharaoh tells of a famous dream of the king in which the land of Egypt was prophesized to experience seven years of plentiful harvest and seven years of horrible drought. And as the book Genesis goes on to tell, this scenario actually played itself out over an agriculturally volatile 14-year period. In fact, some biblical commentators claim that in this story, Pharaoh was actually given a choice of which sequence he wanted to experience first, the seven good years or the seven bad years. Like any good decision maker he decided to go with the good years first. According to legend, he, together with Joseph, who was now promoted to the status of prince as his reward for figuring this all out, managed to store enough grain during the seven good years to withstand the devastating impact of the seven years that followed.

This might be a good analogy for what's in store for baby boomers over the next few years, as they transition into the next stage of their life. As these 75 million people approach their retirement years, they will face a similar dilemma although without the legendary choice given to Pharaoh. Given the relevance of this concept, I dedicate this chapter to illustrating precisely how important it is to get the "good" seven years before the "bad" seven years.

I find it puzzling that although most people I talk to appreciate that good-first is better than bad-first, and many say it is obvious, they apply this gut instinct too broadly and often get the implications wrong. Let me explain with a simple thought experiment.

Assume for a moment that you have $100,000 to invest for a few years. You place this sum in a basic mutual fund that goes on to earn 27% in the first year of ownership so that your investment is worth $127,000 at the end of the first year. Now assume that you hold on to the fund; you don't sell any units or buy any more, and in the second year the same fund increases by a mere 7%. At the end of the second year your investment is now worth $127,000 plus an additional 7%, which is $135,890. Finally in the third year the fund has a very bad year and to your dismay loses 13% of its value. Your investment after three years is now worth 87% of its previous year's value, $118,224. Out of despair and fear, you decide to get out. At least, you say to yourself, you made a total of 18.2% on your original $100,000.

Here is my main point: What happens if I reverse the order of your investment returns and you happen to lose 13% in the first year, you earn 7% in the second year, and you get the 27% only in the third year? Will you end up with more or less than $118,224? Are you worse off since the three years {−13%, +7%, +27%} started on the wrong foot compared to {+27%, +7%, −13%}?

Many people I ask this question to say, "yes." They claim it is worse to experience the loss first. But the indisputable truth is that you will have the exact same amount of money, namely $118,224. If you don't believe me, look at Figure 6.1 and work out the arithmetic. Notice that $100,000 × 1.27 × 1.07 × 0.87 is exactly the same as $100,000 × 0.87 × 1.07 × 1.27. The order is not important when you are buying and holding; no cash flow goes in or out. Indeed, the only thing that matters is the (compound) average of 5.7%. This is exactly why mutual funds tout their 5-, 10-, and 20-year compound returns. The year-by-year numbers don't really matter when all you do is buy and hold.

But, and many of you know this already, if you are withdrawing money from this investment, the order does become relevant, and the earlier the losses, the greater their impact. This is the so-called sequence-of-returns effect. You, like Pharaoh, want the famine returns delayed as long as possible. The objective of this chapter is to illustrate precisely how impactive the sequence of returns can be as we transition into retirement, and why it is so important to think differently about investing as we complete the process of converting our human capital into financial capital.

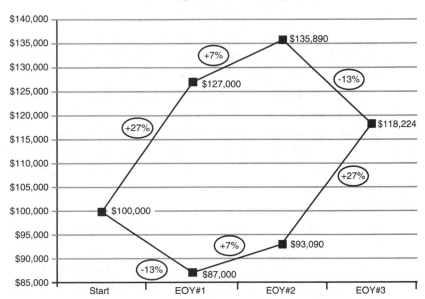

Figure 6.1   The path doesn't matter at all.

Source: Moshe Milevsky and the IFID Centre, 2008.

Retirement Income Trigonometry

Stock markets, interest rates, and investment returns move in periodic cycles. Unfortunately, these cycles, are swamped with noise and become evident only with the benefit of hindsight. The current academic consensus is that they are extremely difficult to predict in advance. Nevertheless, these cycles—once they do materialize—can have a profound impact on the sustainability of retirement income.

If you retire and start to withdraw money from your invested financial capital just as the economy moves into a bear market cycle, your portfolio's longevity can be at risk. Your nest egg will not last as long as it would under an equivalent spending plan that started during a bull market cycle. This observation is often labeled by the term "sequence-of-returns" risk and is used by many in the insurance industry to explain the importance of downside protection during the so-called retirement risk zone—the years just before and just after your wealth accumulation peak illustrated earlier in Figure 1.1.

I would like to illustrate how a bull or bear market cycle can impact the sustainability of your portfolio by appealing to ideas from basic high school trigonometry, also known as the mathematics of sine and cosine waves. And although your skills might be rusty after these many years, the main story should be accessible to all.

First, allow me to review the basic arithmetic of generating income and sustainability. Assume you start retirement with a nest egg of exactly $100 and you allocate this to an investment fund that earns a real (that is, after inflation) 5% per annum during every year of your retirement. For simplicity, I take this 5% to be an annual percentage rate (APR) that compounds continuously over time. Remember, this implies that if inflation is 3% per annum, then your nominal return is (approximately) 5% + 3% = 8%. If inflation is 4%, then your nominal return is (approximately) 9%.

Now let's spend some money. If you withdraw $6 (also inflation adjusted) per year from this portfolio, the nest egg will be exhausted in exactly 35.8 years. In contrast, if you withdraw $7 (inflation adjusted) per year, the funds will last for 25.1 years. If you withdraw $8, the funds will last 19.6 years. Remember, all of this assumes your portfolio earns the same consistent inflation-adjusted 5% APR, for as long as the funds exist.

At this point I need you to suspend your disbelief and imagine a perfectly cyclical (sine wave) financial market—and I mean perfect with no randomness, noise, or real-world uncertainty. I'm going to describe two symmetrically opposed scenarios. Look at Figure 6.2 for a picture that's worth the next 200 words.

In this figure, the smooth middle line represents the path of the investment portfolio, assuming that it earns a constant 5% each and every year and that you are also withdrawing $7 per year on a continuous basis. Let this line serve as our benchmark. In contrast, the solid dark line represents how the portfolio starts out earning an APR of 5% on the first day of retirement. To be exact, this is 2 basis points (or 0.02%) during the first day of retirement, which is a 5% APR divided by 250 trading days. The market then moves into a bull-market cycle so that your annualized returns slowly increase until it peaks at 20% per annum (8 basis point per day) in approximately 19 months. In the language of sine waves, the market peaks after approximately $\pi/2$ years. Remember the Greek letter π is equal to approximately 3.14 years, which is 37.68 months, so $\pi/2$ is just shy of 19 months. Throughout this scenario, $7 per year is also being withdrawn.

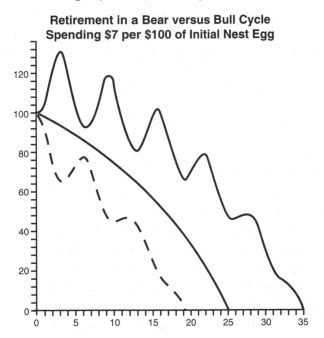

Retirement in a Bear versus Bull Cycle
Spending $7 per $100 of Initial Nest Egg

Figure 6.2 Will your runny nest egg zig before it zags?

Source: M. Milevsky, "The Trigonometry of Retirement Income," *Research Magazine*, February 2007.

Then after hitting this peak, financial markets start to decline so that approximately 19 additional months later the market is back to earning an APR of 5%. It has gone from 5% up to 20% and then down to 5% over approximately 3.14 years.

Bear with me here. Imagine that markets then continue to decline for another 19 months and your portfolio's investment return hits −10% annualized (which is −4 basis points per day). See (the dark solid line in) Figure 6.2 for an illustration of the evolution of this entire cycle from start to finish over 2π (which equals 6.28) years. This sine wave I have constructed exhibits the amplitude (volatility) of plus or minus 15%, and ranges in value from −10% to +20%.

As a perfectly symmetric alternative, consider the scenario, represented by the dashed line, in which you retire and start to withdraw $7 annually, while the market is earning the same 5% per annum, but it immediately moves into a bear-market cycle so that 19 months into retirement you are earning −10% (that is, losing money) per annum, and 19 months later you are back to 5% per annum and 19 months after that you are earning 20%, and so on.

Once again, the two diametrically opposed paths are illustrated in Figure 6.2. All paths earn an average APR of 5% over the long run.

Again, in the absence of any withdrawals, if you only invested $1 at the start of a cycle (up or down, bullish or bearish) then at the end of a market cycle of 2π (which equals 6.28) years, you would have a compound annual return of 5% and the same amount of money: $1.37 in all cases. When you are buying and holding it doesn't matter what path the market takes as long as you get the 5% annualized return! Whether you move up first and then down, or down first and then up, if your compound return is 5%, you will know exactly where you end up. But the situation is very different when you withdraw money.

I trust you would agree that on any given day, week, or month, you don't really know in which direction the market will move over the next few years. It might go north or it might go south. The relevant question is how long your portfolio will last based on the possible starting market cycles. It should be intuitive that your retirement will be worse off if markets go south versus north. But how bad will it be? That's my second point.

Table 6.1 summarizes the main results for cases in which you start retirement with $100 and withdraw $6, $7, or $8 per year on a continuous basis. For example, as you saw in Figure 6.2, if you are withdrawing $7 per year and you are invested in a relatively volatile asset class that fluctuates between +20% and −10%, the portfolio can last anywhere between 34.9 years to 18.9 years depending on where in the cycle you start retirement.

TABLE 6.1 Anything Can Happen; Don't Leave It to Chance

Sequence of Returns		$100 Initial Nest Egg and Spending		
	Market Cycle	*$6 Per Year*	*$7 Per Year*	*$8 Per Year*
N.A.	*Flat 5% Market*	35.8 yrs.	25.1 yrs.	19.6 yrs.
+5,+10,+5,0	*Retire into Bull*	41.7	27.7	21.3
+5,0,+5,+10	*Retire into Bear*	31.4	22.7	18.0
+5,+15,+5,-5	*Retire into Bull*	50.1	31.0	23.4
+5,-5,+5,+15	*Retire into Bear*	27.9	20.8	16.5
+5,+20,+5,-10	*Retire into Bull*	65.6	34.9	25.5
+5,-10,+5,+20	*Retire into Bear*	24.9	18.9	15.4
+5,+25,+5,-15	*Retire into Bull*	*Infinity*	39.6	28.1
+5,-15,+5,+25	*Retire into Bear*	22.4	17.1	14.3

Source: M.Milevsky, "The Trigonometry of Retirement Income," *Research Magazine*, February 2007.

As you can see from the same table, if you invest in even more volatile asset classes that range from +25% to –15% per year, for example, the dispersion of outcomes is an even wider 17.1 years to 39.6 years.

Another important insight from the Table 6.1 is the impact of the spending rate itself. Notice that when you are spending $8 per year, the gap between the "good" sequence and the "bad" sequence of returns is only 21.3 – 18 = 3.3 years in the first rows (low risk) of the table. This same gap is 41.7 – 31.4 = 10.3 years when spending is reduced to $6 per year. At first glance this might seem odd. Why is the sequence-of-returns effect more powerful at lower spending rates? But, of course, this is a relative effect. If you spend more (that is, $8) you will be worse off in terms of sustainability horizon regardless of the sequence, compared to only spending $6 per year. That said, the gap between worst- and best-case scenario increases the less you spend. This impact becomes more pronounced at greater volatility levels. Withdrawing less might improve your sustainability odds somewhat, but it won't immunize you from a bad initial sequence of returns.

For those who are not satisfied by hypothetical scenarios with perfectly cyclical returns, Figures 6.3 and 6.4 illustrate examples that are
more realistic or that resemble real-world conditions. In Figure 6.3,
two hypothetical funds, Fund A and Fund B, follow a seemingly identical "buy and hold" strategy. Both have a starting balance of $100,000
and both earn an identical mean return of 10.4% with the same volatility or standard deviation of 14.6%. Notice that after 20 years, in the
absence of any withdrawals or deposits, the ending value for both accounts is $658,000. Again, returns order in this case has absolutely no
relevance.

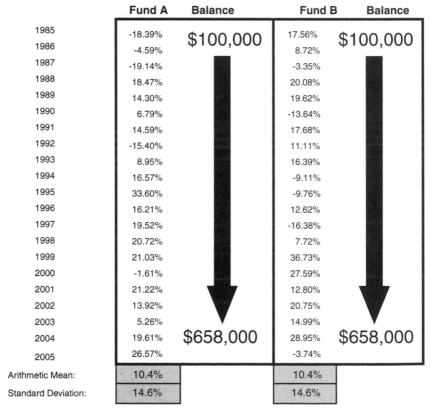

	Fund A	Balance	Fund B	Balance
1985	-18.39%	$100,000	17.56%	$100,000
1986	-4.59%		8.72%	
1987	-19.14%		-3.35%	
1988	18.47%		20.08%	
1989	14.30%		19.62%	
1990	6.79%		-13.64%	
1991	14.59%		17.68%	
1992	-15.40%		11.11%	
1993	8.95%		16.39%	
1994	16.57%		-9.11%	
1995	33.60%		-9.76%	
1996	16.21%		12.62%	
1997	19.52%		-16.38%	
1998	20.72%		7.72%	
1999	21.03%		36.73%	
2000	-1.61%		27.59%	
2001	21.22%		12.80%	
2002	13.92%		20.75%	
2003	5.26%		14.99%	
2004	19.61%	$658,000	28.95%	$658,000
2005	26.57%		-3.74%	
Arithmetic Mean:	10.4%		10.4%	
Standard Deviation:	14.6%		14.6%	

Figure 6.3   Completely different histories, same exact outcome.

Source: Moshe Milevsky and the IFID Centre, 2008.

	Fund A	Balance	Fund B	Balance
1985	-18.39%	$74,606	17.56%	$110,559
1986	-4.59%	$64,183	8.72%	$113,202
1987	-19.14%	$44,898	-3.35%	$102,406
1988	18.47%	$46,189	20.08%	$115,966
1989	14.30%	$45,796	19.62%	$131,714
1990	6.79%	$41,905	-13.64%	$106,743
1991	14.59%	$41,020	17.68%	$118,612
1992	-15.40%	$27,705	11.11%	$124,794
1993	8.95%	$23,184	1 6.39%	$138,246
1994	16.57%	$20,026	-9.11%	$118,654
1995	33.60%	$19,754	-9.76%	$100,069
1996	16.21%	$15,955	12.62%	$105,695
1997	19.52%	$12,070	-16.38%	$81,380
1998	20.72%	$7,571	7.72%	$80,659
1999	21.03%	$2,163	36.73%	$103,287
2000	-1.61%	$0	27.59%	$124,785
2001	21.22%	$0	12.80%	$133,757
2002	13.92%	$0	20.75%	$154,516
2003	5.26%	$0	14.99%	$170,683
2004	19.61%	$0	28.95%	$213,099
2005	26.57%	$0	-3.74%	$198,139
Arithmetic Mean:	10.4%		10.4%	
Standard Deviation:	14.6%		14.6%	

Figure 6.4   Why the difference? The first few years of Investment Returns.

Source: Moshe Milevsky and the IFID Centre, 2008.

As you probably expected by now, the outcome is very different when we try to create a pension from this pot of money, as opposed to just letting it grow. Now imagine you modify the scenario and withdraw $7,000 from both Fund A and Fund B at the end of each year. As you can see in Figure 6.4, Fund A actually runs out of money just before the year 2000, while Fund B ends with a balance higher than the initial deposit of $100,000. A closer look at the actual annual returns once again leads to the same culprit: poor returns during the retirement risk zone in the case of Fund A, compared to the strong initial performance of Fund B. Here is the bottom line: When you are accumulating wealth by buying and holding, the sequence of return will not matter (or will matter much less) compared to when you are no longer saving for retirement.

A Statistical Perspective

Another way to measure the exact impact of an untimely investment "famine" on the sustainability of your retirement income is to analyze many sample retirees who experienced good and bad returns at different points in their retirement, and then see who faired better. We don't have this luxury of data, and it might take a while to see things play out with the baby boomers.

The next best thing to a natural experiment is a diligent research associate with a powerful computer at her disposal. This I have. And together with Anna Abaimova, we generated thousands of possible sample paths for the economic future of a theoretical retirement. We used Monte Carlo techniques—a topic I elaborate upon in Chapter 8, "Spending Your Retirement in Monte Carlo"—to simulate sample paths for inflation, investments returns, health, and longevity. In some of these simulation paths, the hypothetical retiree was "killed" (by the computer algorithm) while still having plenty of money in her retirement account. In other simulation paths, the retiree ran out of money and had to tap other sources of wealth (housing, kids, welfare) to continue spending. The summary results of this analysis are shown in Table 6.2.

TABLE 6.2   Impact of Various "Risk Factors" on Retirement Income Sustainability for a 65-Year-Old (100% Equity Allocation)

Risk Factor	Correlation: Factor and Sustainability
Worse Than Expected Returns During:	
First 7 yrs	−56.3%
Second 7 yrs	−27.5%
Third 7 yrs	−11.0%
Fourth 7 yrs	−2.4%
Fifth 7 yrs	−1.2%
Higher longevity	−53.9%
Higher inflation	−5.8%

Simulation assumptions: neutral spending consumption rate = 9.85%; Equity: expected returns =11%, volatility = 18%; Inflation: expected inflation =3%, volatility = 2%

Source: M. Milevsky, "Feast or Famine First?," *Research Magazine*, December 2007.

Recall from Chapter 3 that the concept of correlation coefficients measures the extent to which two factors move in the same or opposite direction. In the Table 6.2 set of results, first notice how all the correlation coefficients in the table are negative. As you might expect, this means that if you experience worse-than-average portfolio investment returns at any time during your retirement, your income sustainability will be lower than expected. The same goes for increased longevity. If you live longer, you must spend more and experience higher inflation during retirement. They are all risk factors and will have a negative impact. Think of them as the factors that reduce your retirement sustainability.

Notice, for example, that the correlation coefficient for the first seven years is –56.3% while the correlation for the second seven years is only –27.5%. The way to interpret this number is as follows: In the many simulations we generated, some resulted in better-than-expected sustainability and others were worse. In fact, half of the time things were better than expected and half of the time they were obviously worse. Of course, we are definitely not advocating that a 50% probability of financial retirement success is an acceptable Monte Carlo number (it isn't), but rather we are using this neutral 50/50 simulation as the basis for the correlation analysis.

In the cases for which the first seven years (from age 65 to age 72) were lousy, more often than not (roughly 56% of the time) the desired income was not sustainable, and the retiree had to reduce his standard of living. However, if the second seven year's return is lousy (between the 73rd birthday and the 79th birthday), the impact on sustainability is lower: 27% of the time, the income was not sustainable.

Just as interesting is the impact of longevity risk. I return to this important topic in the next chapter, but for now think of longevity risk as the risk that you outlive all of your human and financial capital. Notice that its correlation coefficient is –53.9% in Table 6.2, which is almost as high and important as the impact of the first seven years with a coefficient of –56.3%. In other words, if someone were to ask me, "What has a worse impact on income sustainability? Is it underestimating my life expectancy or getting unlucky in the first few years of retirement?" My answer would be that they are roughly on the same order of magnitude. Be fearful of them both.

Another byproduct of this fact is that some of the old rules of investing—namely that for the same level of investment volatility or risk (as measured by standard deviation), one is better off with a higher return—may no longer apply. One of the fundamental axioms of modern portfolio theory and current investment management is that investments can be ranked solely on the basis of their mean (average) return and variance (volatility).

Stated differently, there is a strong relationship between investments that exhibit a high degree of return variability (that is, they fluctuate a lot) and their long-term growth rate. Variability tends to be measured by standard deviation. This is illustrated in Figure 6.5, where the upper portion of the curve, which is often called the investment frontier, moves higher for greater values of standard deviation. In general, investors are counseled to never accept lower return (for example, 8% compared to 7%) from a product, if the statistical fluctuations of the two products are identical. In retirement, this may no longer be the case since the traditional measures of risk, the daily fluctuations, may not capture the sequence of return risk that I described.

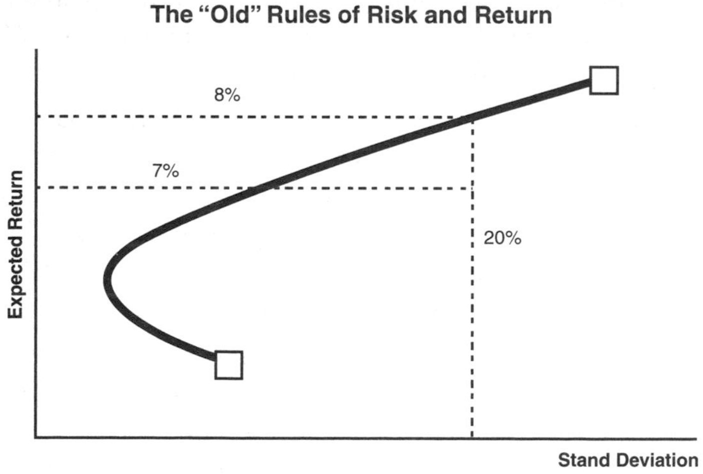

The "Old" Rules of Risk and Return

Figure 6.5   Why would you give up 100 basis points?

Source: Based on work by H.M. Markowitz, "Portfolio Selection," *Journal of Finance*, 1952, 7(1):77-91.

Anyway, the technical details of these regressions can get somewhat numbing but the bottom line here is that the sequence-of-investment-returns effect is real. You must protect yourself against this unique hazard; that is, the risk that you get the seven-year famine before the feast.

Placebos and Mirages

Some commentators have expressed the view that by using a strategy called the "bucket approach to retirement income," they can somehow avoid the damaging impact of a poor sequence of investments returns. Under this strategy one places a few years' worth of retirement spending needs money into safe investments, and then plans on not touching the remaining funds in the event of a bear market. Then, if markets decline, a retiree should simply be counseled to only take income from his bond allocation, then "wait for the stock allocation to recover," and thus avoid selling at a loss. While this strategy might sound good at first, it doesn't hold up to careful scrutiny.

I believe these strategies are an optical illusion at best and create a potential for grave disappointment at worst. If you are unlucky enough to earn a poor sequence of initial returns, so-called bucketing of your retirement income is not a guaranteed bailout. I will try to convince you of this fact using what logicians call a counterexample.

To make this a fair apples-to-apples comparison I will arrange my story so that all else is equal. Thus, I start with two hypothetical retirees: Ms. Stephanie Swip and Mr. Brett Bucket. They both begin their retirement with exactly $100,000 in liquid assets from which they would like to receive or generate $750 per month, in nominal terms, which is $9,000 per annum, for as long as possible. Note that under a fixed 7% investment return per year the funds would only last for about 21 years. Granted, this is a very high and therefore unsustainable spending rate, and I would never counsel either of them to withdraw this much. My objective is not to suggest a prudent spending rate but to examine the impact of two strategic alternatives.

Now, Stephanie chooses to invest her entire $100,000 in one balanced mutual fund that internally has 30% of its assets allocated to risk-free cash instruments and the remaining 70% allocated to diversified equities. This allocation is periodically rebalanced by the fund manager so that Stephanie has a 70/30 equity/cash mix on an ongoing basis at all points in time. I will also assume that this balanced portfolio is expected to earn an arithmetic average of 7% per annum net of all fees. Remember that each month through her systematic withdrawal plan (SWiP), Stephanie liquidates as many units as necessary (more during a bear, less during a bull market) to create the desired income of $750.

In contrast to Stephanie, Brett decides to implement a so-called "buckets" approach to retirement income generation. He places $25,400 of his $100,000 nest egg in cash instruments to cover the next 3 years (36 months) of $750 per month expenses. The remaining $74,600 is invested in a pure equity portfolio that (I am assuming) is expected to earn an average of 8% per annum. This bucket will not be touched or tapped for three years.

I have picked these numbers carefully. Brett has set aside precisely $25,400 because I have assumed cash is yielding a constant and predictable 4.0% per annum. The present value of 36 monthly cash flows of $750 at 4.0% / 12 = 0.333% per month is exactly $25,400. This bucket of cash will generate the desired payments, and Brett will not have to liquidate any stocks (at a loss) if the market takes a tumble during the first three years of withdrawals, which is something I previously described.

Notice that if we focus on the total portfolio held by either Stephanie or Brett at the time of retirement, they both are expecting their total investment portfolio to earn 7% per annum. Stephanie selected a mutual fund that is projected to earn 7%, while Brett has 25.4% (that is, $25,400 / $100,000) allocated to cash earning 4.0% and 74.6% (that is, $74,600 / $100,000) allocated to equities earning 8%. This also works out to an average of 7%.

It is very important to keep track of the total asset allocation because it will have a direct impact on my subsequent arguments. In fact, all these return assumptions—that is, 4% for cash, 8% for equity, and 7% for the balanced fund—were not arbitrary. They were selected so that at the point of retirement Stephanie and Brett have the same initial asset allocation but different dynamic strategies. Otherwise, any comparison is meaningless.

One final assumption that I will now make for the sake of my counterexample, and this one is a bit artificial, is that equities as an asset class will earn one of only three possible investment returns with equal probability. Namely, equities will either earn 8% (the average), earn 35%, or they will lose 19% in any given year. The arithmetic average of these three numbers is exactly 8%; this cycle is illustrated in Figure 6.6. Some of you may have seen this type of handy triangle before.

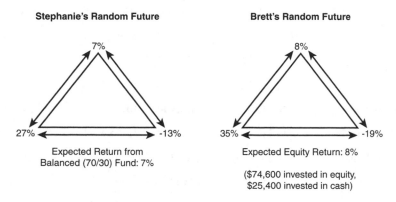

Figure 6.6 Who will be better off?

Source: M. Milevsky, "Spending Buckets and Financial Placebos," *Research Magazine*, June 2007.

The standard deviation of this variable consisting of three possible investment returns is the square root of the expression: $(1/3)(0)+(1/3)(0.27)^2+(1/3)(0.27)^2$, which is approximately 21.9%.

By virtue of the fact that Stephanie has invested in a fund that has 70% in "triangular equities" and 30% in cash (and to be consistent with our previous assumptions), Stephanie's fund will also earn one of three possible investment returns. She will either earn 27% (the good) or she will lose 13% (the bad) or she will earn 7% (the average). All of them have an equal probability of occurring. Note that the standard deviation for her fund's random return is the square root of $(1/3)(0)+(1/3)(0.20)^{\wedge}2+(1/3)(0.20)^{\wedge}2$, which is 16.3%. And, just to convince yourself that the math works out, notice that ($74,600/$100,000) × 21.9% is also 16.3%. In other words, at the point of retirement both of them have an equivalent total asset allocation but a very different strategic plan for how to generate an income during the next three years. Table 6.3 illustrates the possible returns that Stephanie and Brett will encounter.

**TABLE 6.3   You Win Some and You Lose Some:
Brett's "Buckets" and Stephanie's "SWiPs"**

Scenario	Stephanie's Wealth		Brett's Wealth	
Avg, Avg, Avg	{7%,7%,7%}	$93,345	{8%,8%,8%}	**$94,760**
Bad, Bad, Bad	{–13%,–13%,–13%}	**$45,105**	{–19%,–19%,–19}	$41,996
Good, Good, Good	{27%,27%,27%}	$181,854	{35%,35%,35%}	**$210,002**
Avg, Avg, Bad	{7%,7%,–13%}	**$75,509**	{8%,8%,–19%}	$72,247
Avg, Bad, Avg	{7%,–13%,7%}	**$73,757**	{8%,–19%,8%}	$72,247
Bad, Avg, Avg	{–13%,7%,7%}	$71,878	{–19%,8%,8%}	**$72,247**
Bad, Bad, Avg	{–13%,–13%,7%}	**$56,190**	{–19%,–19%,8%}	$55,083
Bad, Avg, Bad	{–13%,7%,-13%}	**$57,942**	{–19%,8%,–19%}	$55,083
Avg, Bad, Bad	{7%,–13%,–13%}	**$59,480**	{8%,–19%,–19%}	$55,083
Avg, Avg, Good	{7%,7%,27%}	$114,813	{8%,8%,35%}	**$123,545**
Avg, Good, Avg	{7%,27%,7%}	$116,920	{8%,35%,8%}	**$123,545**
Good, Avg, Avg	{27%,7%,7%}	$119,180	{35%,8%,8%}	**$123,545**
Good, Good, Avg	{27%,27%,7%}	$148,387	{35%,35%,8%}	**$161,074**
Good, Avg, Good	{27%,7%,27%}	$146,280	{35%,8%,35%}	**$161,074**
Avg, Good, Good	{7%,27%,27%}	$143,528	{8%,35%,35%}	**$161,074**
Bad, Bad, Good	{–13%,–13%,27%}	$69,559	{–19%,–19%,35%}	**$71,815**
Bad, Good, Bad	{–13%,27%,–13}	**$73,405**	{–19%,35%,–19%}	$71,815
Good, Bad, Bad	{27%,–13%,–13%}	**$76,780**	{35%,–19%,–19%}	$71,815
Good, Good, Bad	{27%,27%,–13%}	$120,551	{35%,35%,–19%}	**$122,806**
Good, Bad, Good	{27%,–13%,27%	$116,705	{35%,–19%,35%}	**$122,806**
Bad, Good, Good	{–13%,27%,27%}	$111,681	{–19%,35%,35%}	**$122,806**
Avg, Bad, Good	{7%,–13%,27%}	$90,955	{8%,–19%,35%]	**$94,193**
Avg, Good, Bad	{7%,27%,–13%}	**$94,801**	{8%,35%,–19%}	$94,193
Bad, Avg, Good	{–13%,7%,27%}	$88,667	{–19%,8%,35%}	**$94,193**
Bad, Good, Avg	{–13%,27%,7%}	$90,774	{–19%,35%,8%}	**$94,193**
Good, Avg, Bad	{27%,7%,–13%}	**$96,650**	{35%,8%,–19%}	$94,193
Good, Bad, Avg	{27%,–13%,7%}	**$94,898**	{35%,–19%,8%}	$94,193

Source: M. Milevsky, "Spending Buckets and Financial Placebos," *Research Magazine*, June 2007.

We now get to the interesting part. The way I have set up the counterexample, during the next three years there are 27 distinct economic scenarios that can take place. The 27 comes from three possibilities in the first year, times three in the second year, times three in the third year. Table 6.3 illustrates the 27 scenarios and the value of Stephanie and Brett's portfolio at the end of those three years based on each of those scenarios.

For example, suppose that during the first three years of retirement the stock market goes down for three years in a row. In this case Brett's equity investment of $74,600 loses an annual percentage rate of 19% for three years—mathematically this is a factor of $(1 - 0.19/12)^{\wedge}36$—which is a total 43% destruction in value. As you can see from Table 6.3, after three years of retirement his $74,500 has shrunk to $41,996. And, of course, his cash allocation has been completely spent. In contrast, Stephanie has experienced the same three-year bear market while spending the same $9,000 per year. Her diversified (70/30) fund has lost 13% each year, but she emerges from her three-year SWiP with $45,105, which is not very pretty, but it is better than Brett's situation.

This, of course, is just one of the 27 possible scenarios; but it is a most revealing case. The intuition for this result is as follows. Although Stephanie and Brett start off with the exact same asset allocation, this is not the case at the end of the three years. Because Brett has spent his cash, he is now 100% invested in equities while Stephanie is still holding a balanced 70/30 portfolio. As I discussed in Chapter 3, "Diversification over Space and Time," on the subject of diversification, a 100% exposure to equity is good when markets are going up, but horrible when they are going down. Ergo, you have not protected yourself against a poor sequence of returns—if you consider your total asset allocation.

The table also offers some optimistic news for Brett. If markets increase strongly (35%) for three years in a row, he will end up with $210,002 while Stephanie will only have $181,854. This gap of almost $40,000 is quite impressive and to some might seem to vindicate the buckets approach. But remember, the reason this happens is because Brett implicitly has a more aggressive (equity) asset allocation as he progresses through retirement. All his spending comes from cash. This creates a lopsided rebalancing toward equity.

Of the 27 scenarios in Table 6.3, a total of 16 of them favor Brett and 11 of them favor Stephanie. Yes, there is a 60% chance Brett will be better off and a 40% chance that Stephanie will be better off. Indeed, the odds might favor Brett, but this is not a guaranteed way to avoid a poor sequence of returns. Most importantly, notice that in just about all the scenarios for which the market lost money in the first two or three years, Stephanie is better off than Brett. In other words, Brett is not protected from a prolonged bear market.

What could change our results in the real world as opposed to this hypothetical and stylized example? Of course if both Stephanie and Brett decide to spend less (all else being equal), then they have obviously reduced their exposure to sequence-of-returns risk. In the extreme, if neither of them withdraws any money whenever markets are down, they will have immunized themselves against sequence-of-returns risk.

In sum, adopting the so-called buckets approach to retirement income planning will lead to an increased implicit exposure to equities leading to unpredictable fluctuation over time. Moreover, if indeed you experience a poor initial sequence of investment returns so that you have been forced to liquidate all your cash investments, you might find yourself with a 100% equity exposure well into retirement and possibly deep into a bear market. This is in contrast to the nonbucketer (okay, lousy word) who is maintaining the same exact asset mix and hence the same financial risk profile over time. Sure, the market might recover by the time you have to tap into the equity portion—or it might not.

Either way, the strategy I just described does not allow you to hedge your financial capital against the sequence of returns risk. Safety with the buckets approach is just a mirage.

In addition to some of the purely analytic facts about sequence of returns, there is yet another reason why getting a bear market prior to a bull market, or vice versa, might not make much of a difference, which gets back to our original thesis about human capital. As much as you might hate to admit this, if things do go awfully wrong in the stock market, or in your 401(k) or with any of your investments prior to retirement, you can always delay your retirement and work another year or two. Sure, many of us might want to retire and stop working at the age of 55 or 60. But we have the ability to extract additional human capital and convert this into financial capital. This fact itself gives us the ability to take on more investment risk. It enables you to withstand the potential fluctuations in a way that would not apply in the retirement income phase. Indeed, once you have left the workforce, you no longer have that option.

As the responsibility toward the provision of retirement income shifts from corporations and governments, toward individuals, one is forced to take a more careful look at the management of human capital over the life cycle. Early on in life, we can afford to self-insure (that is, not insure and effectively live with the circumstances of) the risk of the sequence of returns.

Finally, in my opinion, the simplest and easiest way to protect against this new and unique risk that is most relevant to retirees as their human capital has been spent is to purchase or invest in some of the products I describe in Chapter 9, "Annuities Are Personal Pensions." For now, remember that averages can be very deceiving.

Summary

- When you accumulate wealth, and invest for the long run, the exact sequence of investment returns does not matter. One dollar grows to the same amount regardless of whether it earns 10% before the 15% or the other way around.

- But when you withdraw money, the situation is no longer as simple. You can earn a positive average return and still end up exhausting your portfolio early in retirement. Two neighbors can retire at different times, experience the same average rate of return, but still have completely different retirement experiences.

- Getting the right average in the long run might not be enough. This is yet another reason that pensions and other products that are meant to create a pension-like income stream are such an important component of a healthy retirement income portfolio.

Endnotes

The mathematics of retirement income planning can get quite complicated, and for those who are interested in a more advanced treatment I recommend (naturally) the book by Milevsky (2006).

7

Longevity Is a Blessing and a Risk

"...According to the National Centre for Health Statistics, in mid-2007, life expectancy in the U.S. was 77.8 years, so I should plan for about 15 years of retirement...."

Myth #7

The 77.8 number is quite true and one often reads that at the end of the 20th century, life expectancy in the U.S. hit a record high of approximately 73.6 years for males and 79.2 years for females. Based on statistics from the Social Security Administration (SSA), which apply to the U.S. population in its entirety, these numbers have been steadily increasing over time: In 1950 the respective values were 65.6 for males and 71.1 for female. Yet, you might wonder why there is all the fuss about financing a long period of retirement. Yes, people are living longer compared to fifty years ago and they are living healthier, as the recent headlines indicate, such as those shown in Figure 7.1. But can saving enough money during your working years to generate an average of 10 to 15 years of income be that onerous?

Of course, most financial professionals will see through my straw man fallacy and know that these numbers do not apply to their healthier and wealthier clients. More critically, these numbers apply only at birth, not at retirement, and do not account for any possible reductions in future mortality. They are based on today's death and survival rates.

If you are a 75-year-old-male or -female, your life expectancy is much higher than at age zero. In this case, using the same SSA statistics, the numbers are now 84.6 and 86.9, respectively. The headline values—73.6 and 79.2—only apply to newborns. As you age and, hence, survive hazards like infant mortality, teenage accidents, child bearing years, and so on, your life expectancy at these higher ages increases.

Financial Times, January 19, 2004

Figure 7.1   The headlines are changing.

Yet, when talking to individuals who are outside the financial services (or medical) profession, I find that there is pervasive confusion regarding what these life expectancy numbers actually mean. These misunderstandings can lead to behaviors that result in under-saving and underestimates of retirement income needs. In this chapter, I take a closer look and discuss some of the misconceptions as they relate to longevity and the amount of time your financial capital truly must last.

Life Expectancy Is Not That Meaningful

To start off, I think that life expectancy averages are not the best way to explain these ideas. Averages can be deceiving. In fact, there is a silly joke about a statistician who immerses one hand in scalding hot water and the other in freezing ice water, and then declares that the temperature is fine "on average."

I believe that a better way to think about longevity risk and uncertainty is via actuarial probability tables, such as Table 7.1.

TABLE 7.1 Probability of Survival at Age 65

To Age:	Female	Male	At Least One Member of a Male-Female Couple
70	93.9%	92.2%	99.5%
75	85.0%	81.3%	97.2%
80	72.3%	65.9%	90.6%
85	55.8%	45.5%	75.9%
90	34.8%	23.7%	50.3%
95	15.6%	7.7%	22.1%
100	5.0%	1.4%	6.3%

Using a "moderate" mortality assumption.

Data Source: RP2000 Mortality table; IFID Centre calculations.

For example, Table 7.1 shows that if you are a 65-year-old male, using a moderate mortality assumption, there is a greater than 45% chance that you will live to the age of 85. That would obviously require 20 years of retirement income, if you decide to retire exactly at the age of 65. Likewise, the same 65-year-old male has a 24% chance of living to the age of 90, which necessitates 25 years of income. For females the numbers are higher. A female who is 65 years of age has roughly a 35% chance of living to 90. Compare this number to the 24% probability for a male, and you can see the relative impact and magnitude of female longevity. In other words, if you have a large group of 65-year-old males, then slightly less than a quarter of them will live to the age of 90. Of course, we can't know in advance who will be included in that lucky quarter, so to be prudent they all plan for the possibility of 25 years of retirement income. The number increases significantly to 50%, if you consider the chances that at least one member of a male-female couple will survive to age 90.

Another way to think about longevity risk is by interpreting the risk in a more pessimistic manner. Indeed, according to the same actuarial tables, the probability that a 65-year-old male does not reach the age of 70 is approximately 8%. This mortality rate comes from subtracting the listed survival rate of 92.2% from the total of 100%. Yet, as you can see, there is the same 8% chance that he reaches age 95. One group gets 30 years while the other group doesn't even get 5 years. They are of equal odds. This is longevity risk.

Now is a good time for me to reemphasize the fact that there are many possible mortality assumptions or actuarial tables. For example, the Social Security Administration uses very different tables for calculating benefits and projecting future deficits and liabilities. This is because they work with the population as a whole as opposed to a subset of possibly healthier and longer-lived pensioners. In the opposite direction, if you are ever interested in purchasing an immediate life or income annuity, a topic that I discuss in Chapter 9, "Annuities Are Personal Pensions," the insurance company actuaries will use a completely different table. The annuity table assumes much higher survival odds when determining how long you are projected to live and, hence, how much you are to be paid for the rest of your life. This is another example of the effect of asymmetric information, which I discussed in Chapter 2, "Insurance Is a Hedge for Human Capital." In fact, there are so many possible actuarial tables that I often joke that they are like snowflakes; no two are ever alike.

Do People Understand the Odds?

Interestingly, when it comes to identifying factors that we perceive to be the most likely to cut our lifespan short, a study published by LIMRA in 2004 suggests that many of us make errors. The study subjects were asked to estimate the probability that they will die because of a number of natural and unnatural causes listed in Table 7.2. Compare the responses in the Estimate column compared to those in the Actual column. The results suggest that people have the tendency to underestimate their chances of dying from natural causes such as heart disease and significantly overestimate their chances of dying from such events as accidents or homicide. Errors in our perception of our expected remaining lifetime, of course, can be detrimental to retirement planning, because a lack of a proper hedging strategy against longevity risk can lead to a retirement income gap that might be difficult to fill.

TABLE 7.2   What Will Be Your Cause of Death?

	Estimate	Actual
Heart Disease	22%	34%
Cancer	18%	23%
Other Natural	33%	35%
Accident	32%	5%
Homicide	10%	1%
Other Unnatural	11%	2%
TOTAL	126%	100%

Source: Life Insurance Marketing Research Association (LIMRA) Survey 2004.

On the other hand, factors that are likely to improve longevity are continuously being studied and, in addition to data that I have summarized in Chapter 2, there are some fascinating findings emerging from demographers, biologists, and gerontologists. This is a topic of ongoing and continuing research. According to a recent study by the U.S. Society of Actuaries (www.soa.org), there are actually twelve factors that affect or influence retirement mortality. They are

- Age
- Gender
- Race and Ethnicity
- Education
- Income
- Occupation
- Marital status
- Religion
- Health behaviors
- Smoking
- Alcohol consumption
- Obesity

In other words, the knowledge of any one of these factors can help predict or better estimate your retirement mortality rate, sometimes by a factor of 2-to-1.

As just one example of these factors, the Max Planck Institute in Germany has recently confirmed, using a large database of actual mortality experience, that although males in general don't live as long as females, interestingly, married males tend to live longer than single males. But oddly enough marriage is not associated with greater longevity for females. For them, being widowed, single, or divorced is a factor associated with reduced mortality. The findings are summarized in Table 7.3 and are quite controversial, besides being somewhat amusing. Why is marriage "better" for males' longevity compared to females' longevity? Does this study apply broadly across different demographic groups? The research is still ongoing.

TABLE 7.3 What Reduces Your Retirement Mortality Rates (Beyond the Obvious)?

All Genders	Parents Lived Beyond Age 75
	Mentally Active During Retirement
Male Only	Being Married
Female Only	Being Single, Divorced, or Widowed

Source: Rasmus Hoffmann, "Do Socioeconomic Mortality Differences Decrease with Rising Age?", *Max Planck Institute for Demographic Research*, 2005.

Along the same lines, Table 7.4 displays data showing that life expectancy at age 70 is related to one's income level. Falling within the 80th versus the 20th income percentile can mean the difference of three years in life expectancy for a healthy male or female. The wealthy are healthier.

TABLE 7.4 Health and Wealth: Life Expectancy at Age 70

Income Percentile	Healthy Male	Healthy Female
20th	78.2 yrs	83.8 yrs
40th	79.1 yrs	84.8 yrs
60th	80.1 yrs	85.9 yrs
80th	81.2 yrs	87.0 yrs

Source: Federal Reserve Bank of Chicago, WP 2005-13 (De Nardi, French, and Jones).

As I emphasized in Chapter 2 on the topic of life insurance, please do not confuse the statistical relationship between these factors and actual causality. We are not sure exactly what causes this relationship and whether other factors are at play that impact the link between wealth and longevity, or marital status and longevity. All we can say for certain is that mortality rates are lower among these groups of people. Once again, from a practical perspective, if you are a member of the groups identified as having more favorable mortality experience, you likely should plan for a much longer retirement compared to the average person in the population.

Even status has been linked with an increased life expectancy. Table 7.5 displays the results of a study that examined the impact on life expectancy of being nominated for a particular award versus actually winning it. The difference can mean as much as an extra four years of life.

TABLE 7.5   Status of a Long Life

# of Extra Years	Control Group
3.9	Win Academy Award versus being nominated
1.4	Win Science Nobel prize versus being nominated
2.8	Win Chemistry Nobel versus being nominated

Source: D. Redelmeier and S.M. Singh, *Annals of Internal Medicine*, 134(10):955; M.D. Rablen and A.J. Oswald, Warwick Economic Research Papers, January 2007.

Just as important as the wide variation in longevity estimates depending on the group in question, for any given group, it is virtually impossible to predict what these numbers will look like 10 or 20 years from now. Will some pharmaceutical company discover a drug that eliminates most cancers or heart disease, which will then add five to ten years of life? Or will the epidemic of adult obesity continue to erode public health and thus reduce longevity probabilities? Once again the experts can't answer these questions with any degree of accuracy; this is yet another aspect of what is called aggregate longevity risk.

TABLE 7.6   Chasing Your Life Expectancy

	At Birth	At Age 75
Male	73.6	84.6
Female	79.2	86.9

Source: Life Tables for the United States Social Security Area 1900–2100 Actuarial Study
No. 116.

What is the take-away point from all of these numbers? The most important one is to realize that you are chasing your life expectancy as you age. Table 7.2 summarizes this point once again using U.S. Social Security tables. Don't confuse or misunderstand the numbers you see mentioned and quoted by the media. The next point is that you need to recognize and understand the concept of longevity risk. For those who prefer pictures to numbers, Figure 7.2 provides a graphical illustration of this risk. Although there is a 60% to 80% chance you will spend 10 to 20 years in retirement, there is a 10% to 20% chance you might get to the high 90s or perhaps even triple digits. It's a matter of probabilities. This is a risk. Recall that the opposite risk is premature death that must be hedged using some sort of insurance or risk management strategy.

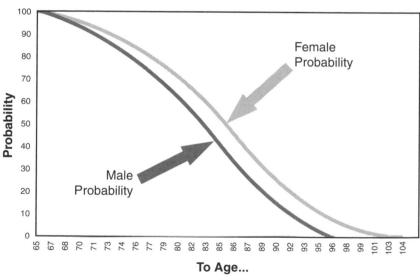

Figure 7.2   Aging down a curved slope.

Data Source: RP2000, SoA; IFID Centre calculations.

Again, when you are young you should take a "long" position in mortality risk. This means that you should be buying or acquiring insurance investments that pay off if and when your mortality rate jumps up unexpectedly. And when you are old, you should reverse the hedge and take a "short" position in mortality. If these is a downward shock and your mortality rate declines, and you, therefore, live longer, you face the risk that your nest egg will not suffice or provide enough income to last for the rest of your life. Note that going short mortality in your old age is the equivalent of buying or purchasing some sort of longevity insurance, which is a topic I return to in Chapter 9.

You need a longevity risk management strategy. You need to develop a plan for the possibility of 30 to 40 years of retirement. As you can see from Table 7.7, more than 73,000 Americans above the age of 100 are alive today. Are you one of them? Will you be one of them?

TABLE 7.7   Longevity Nation

Number of Americans...	
> Age 90	2,000,000
> Age 100	73,000

Source: U.S. Fed News (5 September 2007) based on Census.

Summary

- You chase your life expectancy as you age. The average life expectancy numbers of 77 for males and 80 for females you might see in the newspapers apply at birth only. Healthier, wealthier, and more educated individuals tend to have lower mortality rates and better longevity.

- When you reach your retirement years, in good health and wealth, there is a high probability you will reach the advanced 90s. There is a nontrivial chance you will reach triple digits, and the odds are better for females.

- Our inability to precisely know how long we are going to live and spend in retirement falls under the label of "longevity risk." As the evidence I presented in Chapter 1, "You, Inc.," regarding pension plans illustrated, this is a risk that companies are running away from in droves.

- Personal longevity is a risk-management issue. You must have a strategy in place.

Endnotes

A great book that addressed the entire topic of longevity projections is the book by Olshansky and Carnes (2001). Alternatively, you might want to spend some time browsing the Society of Actuaries website, www.soa.org, where there are many helpful and interesting articles on the topic of mortality and longevity estimates.

8

Spending Your Retirement in Monte Carlo

"…I am getting older, closer to retirement and can't afford to take financial chances, so I am going to invest my money in bonds…."

Myth #8

I've already mentioned one of the most widely cited general rules in the field of retirement investment planning: that the percentage of your portfolio that should be invested in the stock market is 100 minus your age. So, if you are 70 years old, you should only have 30% in the stock market, by 80 you should only have 20%, and so on. Some recent variants of this rule have upped the number 100 to 110 or even 115, but the same idea applies. According to this thinking, your age is the most important determinant. Indeed, I have spent a good amount of time and effort in this book trying to dispel this idea on various levels. Yet, at retirement, the impact of age on asset allocation becomes a very controversial issue.

The debate on this issue is divided. On the one hand, retirees supposedly have a shorter investment horizon and, therefore, incur the risk of not being able to recover from losses in the early stage of retirement by owning a portfolio heavily weighted in equities. On the other hand, by shifting the retirees' investment assets to fixed-income products, especially with current interest rates at historically low levels, the resulting lower income stream could potentially jeopardize their standard of living.

In this chapter, I use some ideas and concepts from recent advances in statistics that fall under the general label of Monte Carlo techniques, to provide yet another perspective on the problem of generating a sustainable retirement income.

Conducting a Needs Analysis

Obviously, before I begin any discussion of retirement investment strategies, you must determine the extent to which you are dependent on your financial assets to sustain a standard of living. In other words, you must conduct a "needs analysis." Pertinent questions would include: What standard of living would you like to maintain during your retirement years? Do you want to travel the world? Will you stay at home? These questions may not be as easy to answer as they seem. They certainly involve making important assumptions about lifestyle preferences and market conditions. But the bottom line is that you—possibly with the help of a financial advisor—must estimate how much you will require on an annual basis to maintain a desired standard of living in retirement. Ideally, this "needs analysis" should be conducted many years prior to retirement while you are still in the process of converting your human capital into financial capital.

The objective is to get a desired number—an annual income level—that can be funded by the total financial assets that you have "mined" from your human capital over your working years (and possibly beyond). Without a good feel for what you'll need, it's meaningless to talk about appropriate investments to finance those needs.

When the needs analysis is completed, you can move on to stage two. There you and your financial advisor can discuss an appropriate asset allocation during the retirement years.

Now, at the risk of sounding simplistic, I'd like to start this analysis by stating the obvious. If, at age 65, you have liquid financial assets that are 100 times greater than your annual consumption requirements, then no matter how you invest during your retirement years, you will never run out of money. Of course, very few Americans are fortunate enough to be in this category. But presumably, those who are have no reason to change their investment philosophy at retirement.

Furthermore, if at age 65 you have liquid financial assets that are only five times greater than your desired annual income level, then you are, quite frankly, doomed. You certainly won't be able to invest or gamble your way out of this conundrum.

With these polar opposites out of the way, I am ready to address the question of an appropriate asset mix to support a desired annual consumption requirement. In other words, given a desired standard of living, what asset allocation—or mix between stocks, bonds, and short-term reserves, such as money market funds—will minimize the probability that you will run out of money during your retirement years?

Let's look at some hypothetical numbers. You have just retired at age 65 with a fairly decent Social Security and company pension, which should provide a large portion of consumption needs on an annual basis. In addition, after many years of contributing financial capital to a 401(k), IRA, or 403(b) plan, you have managed to build a nest egg of approximately $200,000, which is currently sitting in an assortment of mutual funds, term deposits, and other minor investments. The house, fortunately, is fully paid for, and you have no other major liabilities.

After conducting a needs analysis, taking full account of lifestyle choices and retirement plans, you have determined that you require, in addition to your pension, approximately $10,000 every year for the rest of your life. Let's call this the income gap, which is illustrated in Figure 8.1. Naturally, the hope is that the nest egg will be able to provide this additional amount.

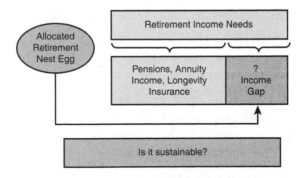

Figure 8.1   Will your nest egg fill the income gap?

Source: Moshe Milevsky and the IFID Centre, 2008.

Before continuing, I should clarify what I mean by $10,000 per year. This estimate assumes that today's prices on which you based your needs will remain the same throughout retirement. In other words, it assumes that the inflation rate for goods and services will be zero for the next 30 years. Rather unrealistic, I'm sure you'd agree. True, inflation has averaged less than 3% almost every year since 1991. But there is no guarantee that the rate will not increase.

Indeed, economic history teaches us that price inflation can resurface suddenly and dramatically. And of course, as I discussed in Chapter 5, "Personal Inflation and the Retirement Cost of Living," the projected inflation rate for retirees might be higher than the general inflation rate for the population at large. Think of the cost of geriatric medical care over the years.

Therefore, a better way to deal with long-term planning (given inflation uncertainty) is to budget and state your needs in real, after-inflation terms. At the same time, you must also project your investment returns in real, after-inflation terms. Let me explain.

As I said earlier, you essentially want to consume $10,000 of today's dollars for the rest of your life. By real consumption, I mean that you will consume $10,000 in your 65th year, $10,000 adjusted by the first year's inflation rate in your 66th year, $10,000 adjusted by the first and second years' inflation rate in your 67th year, and so on. So for example, if the inflation rate for these three years was 2%, 3%, and 4% respectively, then you would consume $10,000 in your 65th year, $10,000*(1+.02) in your 66th year, and $10,000*(1+0.02)*(1+0.03) in your 67th year.

However, to keep things in balance, when I talk about what invested money can earn, I will look at returns in after-inflation terms as well, to account for the fact that your needs were expressed in the same framework.

Ideally, the pension payments come with some form of inflation protection—or indexing—as well. The indexing can be implicitly tied to the consumer price index (CPI), or implicitly tied to the performance of some investment fund.

Practically speaking, the easiest way to get at the $10,000 that you will need each year (about $833 per month) is to set up a systematic withdrawal plan that sells an appropriate number of stocks, mutual funds, or bonds each month to create the desired cash flow. This is like a reverse dollar-cost averaging strategy. Instead of buying an arbitrary number of units with a fixed amount of cash each month, you are selling an arbitrary number of units to create a fixed amount of revenue each month. Then, to account for any price inflation in your consumption needs, you increase the amount withdrawn under the systematic plan on a yearly basis.

Now, before proceeding, we must deal with one other unpleasant aspect of financial budgeting for retirement—income taxes. Your estimate of $10,000 per year probably does not account for income taxes. If this is the case, then the $10,000 that you plan to consume is really an after-tax amount. The pre-tax withdrawal will, therefore, be higher. Everything you pull out of your tax-sheltered plan will be taxed at your marginal tax bracket because you have never actually paid income tax on that money (for the most part). Now, of course, there are also Roth versions of an IRA in which taxes have been paid upfront; the investments then grow tax sheltered but you are exempt from paying income taxes when you withdraw the funds. I won't get into this.

What this all boils down to is that if you require $10,000 to live on—and you are in a 33.33% marginal income tax bracket, for example—then you will really have to withdraw $15,000 from the nest egg, two-thirds of which you will be able to consume yourself. (Just to err on the conservative side, I'm not factoring in certain expenses—for example, medical expenses—that might be tax-deductible.)

Now, a Pandora's box that I would certainly like to avoid is the whole question of what marginal tax brackets will be 10 or 20 years from now. Today, we know that the highest marginal tax bracket is in the 30% to 40% range. But who's to say that federal and state authorities won't raise that number, especially as it applies to funds withdrawn from a tax-sheltered savings plan? In fact, on a professional level, I feel much more confident predicting the long-term expected rate of return from various asset classes than I do predicting what the income tax structure will look like in 15 years. We might move toward a flatter tax system, in which all income is taxed at roughly the same rate, or we might see an increase in progressivism, which would raise tax rates on the top income bracket above the current 30% to 40% region. Unfortunately, it's probably one of the biggest question marks in the financial planning equation. Nevertheless, we must play the game of life based on the current rules, and we must, therefore, make plans based on the current tax system.

By this point, you should have a good sense of your needs, and those needs should be specified on a pretax basis. In the example we've been using, you have $200,000 in a tax-sheltered plan and will need to withdraw $16,000 annually, in after-inflation, pretax terms.

Roughly speaking, therefore, your Needs-to-Wealth (abbreviated as NtW) ratio is $16,000/$200,000 = 8%. Another way of looking at it is to say that your annual income needs represent 8% of the initial wealth available to support those needs. Thus, if you had $400,000 and your needs were 32,000, you would also have an 8% Needs-to-Wealth ratio. This ratio is important because it gives you a general sense of what kind of investment returns you will require to support your annual needs. I would argue that all people—at age 65—with an 8% NtW ratio are more or less in the same boat. That's because whether they have $1,000,000 or a mere $100,000 at retirement, they all have the same relative needs.

We are now ready to revisit the main question. Is $200,000 enough to support $16,000 in annual needs? The answer, of course, really depends on how you invest the $200,000. Another way of asking the question is, can you sustain an NtW ratio of 8%? The answer to this question clearly depends on the holy grail of asset allocation. In other words, it depends on what your investment portfolio looks like during your retirement years.

First of all, let's examine the scenario in which you, as a retiree, will live on the interest and dividends alone. In this case, the $200,000 will have to generate exactly 8% annually to create $16,000—after inflation and before taxes. Unfortunately, money market instruments will earn nowhere near that amount. So, you have a clear choice: 1) invest in these relatively safe investments, knowing that you eventually will have to liquidate your capital and may run out of money or 2) invest a bit more aggressively, and hopefully build your capital instead. Or, of course, you can always decide to reduce consumption.

The math is relatively simple. If your money earns a fixed 5% in real terms, and you consume $16,000 in real terms every year, you will run out of money in about 20 years. That's because the present value of $16,000, discounted at the rate of 5%, is exactly equal to $200,000.

Stated differently, a $200,000 mortgage, amortized at a rate of 5%, will be paid off in exactly 20 years, when the annual payments add up to $16,000.

Okay, you say to yourself, if you can earn a consistent 5% every year in real terms, your money will last for exactly 20 years. That's plenty of time, right?

Well, maybe, or maybe not. Remember, statistics tell us that, using moderate estimates, a 65-year-old man has a 46% chance of living for 20 more years; a 65-year-old woman has a 56% chance of living for 20 more years. So let's put two and two together and see what happens. If they earn 5%, they will run out of money in 20 years. That much is clear. But there's a 46% chance (56% for women) of living for 20 more years. In other words, there is a 46% (56%) chance of outliving your money, if you earn 5% each and every year. Why? Well, the odds of outliving your money are the odds of being alive when the money runs out. If you know exactly when the money will run out, and you know the odds of living to that point, put them together and you have the odds of outliving your money.

Similarly, if your $200,000 nest egg earns a fixed 4% in real terms, you will run out of money even sooner—in about 18 years—because you are earning less. And the odds of living for 18 more years are, not surprisingly, higher than the odds of living for 20 more years. The chances are 54% for men and 63% for women. So if you earn 4% every year, the odds of running out of money are 54% and 63%, respectively.

Another way of saying this is that slightly less than one of every two men (and six of every ten women) will outlive $200,000 invested at 4%, if your annual pretax needs are $16,000.

Again, here's the procedure: Simply compute when the money will run out and then look at the probability of being alive at that time. The higher the number, the more likely it is that your standard of living is simply not sustainable.

The same formula applies in the other direction. If your capital base can earn 6% in real terms, you won't run out of money for 24 years. For a 65-year-old, 24 years might seem far out in the future. Indeed, men at that age have only a 28% chance of living that much longer (and running out of money); women have a 39% chance. These probabilities are lower, but not entirely comforting, especially for women.

Finally, if you are lucky or smart enough to have your capital earn 8% each year—you'll notice it works out to $16,000 each year—you will never run out of money.

Another way to think of this is that a $200,000 mortgage, amortized at 8%, with annual payments of $15,000, will never be paid off. You will barely manage to pay the interest, let alone pay down the principal.

So what are the odds of running out of money when your capital earns 8% every year? Well, I hope you see that they are zero for both men and women. In fact, even if you earned slightly less— 7.75% each year—you would run out of money in about 46 years. And the odds of being alive then are virtually zero for both genders.

No great secrets here: The less you earn, the sooner your money will run out, assuming that you'll need $16,000 in real terms each year.

Incidentally, all of these calculations can be easily performed with the aid of a calculator or spreadsheet, and then you can examine the odds from a mortality table. This calculation is essentially a mortgage amortization schedule that tells you when the money will run out, as opposed to when the mortgage will be paid off.

Table 8.1 returns to a familiar figure and puts a different spin on mortality statistics by looking at when your money will run out, and then stating the probability of living to that age.

What does this chart reveal? Well, for one thing, as we just saw, it tells us that if (at age 65) your financial plan is only valid for 20 years (age 85), there's a 55.8% chance for women (45.5% for men) that you'll still be alive when you run out of money. This is the probability of outliving wealth. It is the probability of still being alive when there is no more money in the account.

Now, at some point, of course, you would realize that you are about to run out of money and would consequently lower your annual consumption. In fact, as you might have been thinking, social support payments would have kicked in long before disaster struck. Or your children might lend financial support. Nobody, in other words, really faces the prospect of starvation.

**TABLE 8.1   Great Numbers Are Worth Repeating:
The Probability of Survival at Age 65**

To Age:	Female	Male
70	93.9%	92.2%
75	85.0%	81.3%
80	72.3%	65.9%
85	55.8%	45.5%
90	34.8%	23.7%
95	15.6%	7.7%

Using a "moderate" mortality assumption.

Data Source: RP2000 Mortality table; IFID Centre calculations.

I would definitely have to agree that in reality this would never happen. Certainly, nobody would withdraw that final year's sum of $16,000 and then say, "Oops, what do I do next year?" But the idea is to plan ahead and to realize the consequences of your actions in their most drastic, worst-case scenarios. To avoid a potential crisis, you must do one of two things, at this point:

- Reassess your asset allocation to determine whether your total capital allocation would permit you to invest more aggressively so that you earn more return on your nest egg

- Cut down on your consumption—in other words, reduce your needs

But here is the $200,000 question. What if you don't know exactly what your rate of return will be? In an ideal world, everyone would know the rate of return for every asset class and the exact rate of inflation during retirement; therefore, you could figure out precisely when your money would run out.

So how can we perform this exercise in the real world, where market returns fluctuate on a daily basis and the length of a human lifespan is so uncertain?

Well, here is where a different set of probabilities come in. We are now ready for the full-fledged model. I call it the "Dual Uncertainty Model" because two sources of uncertainty must be dealt with here: future investment returns and mortality rates.

Table 8.2 averages male and female mortality for simplicity and examines the probability that a given needs-to-wealth ratio is sustainable when market returns and life spans are random.

TABLE 8.2   What Is the Probability That Spending Is Sustainable?

Monte Carlo Simulation Results

Retirement Age	Needs-to-Wealth Ratio				
	5.0%	6.0%	7.0%	8.0%	9.0%
55	71.3%	60.4%	50.1%	41.0%	33.3%
65	83.2%	74.7%	65.9%	57.3%	49.5%
75	93.9%	89.5%	84.2%	78.3%	72.3%

Simulation assumptions: Moderate mortality assumptions;
Equity: expected returns =7%, volatility = 20%
Source: Moshe Milevsky and the IFID Centre, 2008.

Your question at this point, of course, is how and where did I come up with these numbers? I'm glad you asked. I borrowed a technique developed by scientists over the last few decades to deal with complicated questions in nuclear physics. These days, it's used in everything from traffic control to designing better soap. It's called the method of Monte Carlo simulation. We used this method in earlier chapters; now let me explain how it works in more detail.

Together with some colleagues at the Individual Finance and Insurance Decisions (IFID) Centre in Toronto, Canada, we constructed a computer program that generates millions of different scenarios for the financial markets and human mortality. Figure 8.2 illustrates how three of these scenarios or paths might have looked. It is, if you like, the ultimate imagination machine. In one scenario you live to the ripe old age of 97; in another scenario you live to age 86. Some scenarios show the stock market booming for the next 20 years; others indicate a 10-year bear market.

As you might know, simulations of future market behavior have been employed quite successfully in corporate risk management, when a company wants to compute the probability of losing a specific amount of money over a particular time horizon. Government regulators also use the Monte Carlo method to estimate and measure the stability of financial systems.

Figure 8.2   Anything can happen….

Source: Moshe Milevsky and the IFID Centre, 2008.

As you might have guessed, the name Monte Carlo itself comes from the underlying roulette wheel in the computer that generates the different scenarios. It may sound a bit removed to let a computer determine what the future will look like. But in fact, with its exhaustive computing capability, it does cover all possible contingencies, every possible scenario of what could happen over the next 40 years.

True, no computer could have predicted the collapse of the Asian economies a few years ago, or the debt default of the Russian government. The point is not to identify or predict specific events; rather, it is to compute all possibilities for the evolution of the financial markets in conjunction with human mortality.

In one scenario, the computer predicted that the U.S. stock market would fall by 15% in one month. The computer certainly didn't give a reason. It didn't explain why that would happen. It simply said that it was within the realm of possibility. And lo and behold, during August of 1998, the S&P 500 index fell by roughly that amount. Quite uncanny!

Obviously, this doesn't mean that the computer actually predicted the future. It simply means that, using the Monte Carlo simulation, it computed a remote possibility of the market's declining by 15% in one month—and, implicitly, recommended that we should plan for such a possibility. I don't want to alarm you unnecessarily, but in a few scenarios it generated drops even scarier than 25%. Fortunately, the computer estimated the odds of such events to be very small.

Now comes the fun part. After leaving the computer on all night, running millions of these future scenarios, we returned in the morning and started counting.

Specifically, for every possible asset allocation, we counted the number of times that the 65-year-old who starts out with $200,000 and consumes $16,000 per year will run out of money before she dies. These are the people who (theoretically) run out of money. The remaining people, who die with wealth, have managed to avoid outliving their money. The ratio of the former to total number of trials provides us with the probability of outliving your money. We then sift through the cases to locate the asset allocation that minimizes the probability of outliving wealth.

Let's look at an example. In one simulation, a 65-year-old who invested all of his capital in the stock market—consuming $16,000 real dollars each year—ran out of money in roughly five years because he had the uncanny bad luck of investing right before a horrendous (computer-generated) bear market. Again, however, the computer assigned a very low probability to this event.

In another scenario, we found that a 55-year-old was able to take very early retirement, with only $200,000 in wealth, and still manage to consume $16,000 per year for life, by investing completely in equities. But this is because the computer killed him off at age 68, long before his full life expectancy. The computer also assigned this event—a robust stock market combined with early death—a very low probability. Overall, the chance that a 55-year-old man who retires at age 45 with only $200,000 will be able to support a spending habit of $16,000 per year is not great.

Before I go further, I must emphasize the assumptions that go into such a Monte Carlo simulation study. First, I made a moderate assumption about human longevity patterns. If you believe that you are healthier than the average American, then your probabilities of sustainability or success are even lower than the preceding estimates. Remember, if you are healthier than average, then a different mortality table (representing a selected healthy population group) might apply to you. In this case you might be more likely to live much longer and consume longer. All else being equal, this reduces the chances of sustainability.

Second, I assumed in the simulation that the real, after-inflation rate of return from equity markets would be 7% with a volatility of 20%. These numbers correspond with the behavior of American equity markets during the last fifty years. Please note: I am not assuming that you will earn 7% in real terms each year. Rather, I'm assuming that in the long term, you'll earn an average of 7% per annum, with a volatility of 20%. (Remember that volatility is a measure of how wide the spectrum of investment returns is expected to be. Again, a volatility number of 20% means that 95% of the time, the returns will be within $2 \times 20\% = 40\%$ of the expected value.) Admittedly, 7% may be a bit aggressive; a variety of financial commentators believe that the equity risk premium, as it is called, will be much less than observed in the past.

Do I Need a Supercomputer?

No, you don't. In fact, one of the achievements I'm most proud of is a one-line formula that I developed and then published a few years ago with some colleagues of mine that eliminates the need for cumbersome and expensive retirement income computer simulations in many (although not all) cases. Yes, the hunting trophy on my mantle is a mathematical relationship that arrives at the probability of retirement sustainability, given a spending and an investing strategy. To arrive at the reverse statistic, or the probability that a strategy is not sustainable, the former value simply has to be subtracted from 1. So a 40% chance of sustainability in turn implies a 60% chance of "retirement ruin."

The mathematical formula attempts to relate three retirement risk factors—inflation, investment/sequence of returns, and longevity risks—into a summary risk measure called the probability of sustainability. It generalizes the deterministic calculation (which had no uncertainty) at the beginning of this chapter, from constant numbers to random numbers.

To use this formula, you need to have a number of handy input factors or numbers. First, you need the estimated halfway mark for your retirement in years. This is the median remaining lifespan, which is denoted in the formula by MRL. You can get this number from a longevity or mortality table. If you can't find it, ask your doctor or insurance agent. In fact, my MRL is currently 40 years. This number doesn't necessarily imply that I am only planning to live for 40 more years, but rather that half my current cohort of 40-year-olds will reach the age of 80, while half will not.

Another important input factor is your planned inflation-adjusted retirement spending rate. Again, this factor or number is usually denoted in percentage terms; for example, 5% or 6% or 7% of your retirement nest egg. The third and fourth inputs you need for computing the probability of sustainability are (1) the anticipated inflation-adjusted risk and (2) return from your investment portfolio. I denote the expected return by the label AM and the volatility by the label VOL.

So, to start, make sure you have these four numbers handy; for example, 40 years (for median remaining lifespan), 5% spending (for retirement spending rate), 10% (for the annual expected rate of return on investments), and 20% (for volatility of your investments).

The following mathematical definition takes these four input factors—MRL, SPENDING, AM, VOL—and maps them into two summary variables. The summary variables are denoted by "alpha" and "beta" and defined in Figure 8.3.

Retirement Alpha and Beta

$$\alpha = \frac{2 \times AM + 2.773/MRL}{VOL^2 + 0.6931/MRL} - 1$$

$$\beta = \frac{2 \times S}{VOL^2 + 0.6931/MRL}$$

Figure 8.3   The only equations you need for sustainable spending.

Source: M. Milevsky, "Sustainability and Ruin," *Research Magazine*, June 2007.

Finally, use the calculated retirement alpha and retirement beta variables and look up the relevant number under the row and column from Table 8.3 to arrive at the retirement sustainability probability. Remember, there are four inputs that you need to compute or calculate the retirement alpha and beta variables. The spending rate is denoted by the letter S. The average return you expect to earn from your investment portfolio is denoted by the letters AM, which stands for arithmetic mean. The average amount of time you spend in retirement is denoted by the letters MRL, which stands for median remaining lifetime, and the final variable is the investment volatility, denoted by the abbreviation VOL.

So, once again, start with *four* numbers. Convert them into *two* numbers. Then reduce that into *one* number, which is the sustainability of your strategy.

I know this might appear confusing at first, so here are some examples that convert four numbers into two and then into one. Let's imagine that I decide to retire today at the age of 40, when my median remaining lifespan (MRL) is exactly 40 years. Remember that this implies a 50% chance I'll get to age 80. Now assume that I invest whatever nest-egg I have today into a portfolio that is expected to earn an arithmetic average (AM) of 8% after inflation in any given year and that the volatility (VOL) of my portfolio's return is 20%. These numbers—which are on the optimistic side—can usually be estimated from the historical performance of my investments and my current asset allocation. Finally, I desire an annual spending rate of 5% adjusted for inflation. Remember, this means that if I start with $1,000,000, then I'm spending $50,000 per year, and if I start with $100,000, then I'm spending $5,000 per year. Both figures are adjusted annually for inflation.

TABLE 8.3   What Is Your Retirement's Probability of Sustainability?

α/β	0.25	0.50	0.75	1.00	1.25	1.50	1.75	2.00	2.25	2.50	2.75
4.00	100%	100%	99%	98%	96%	93%	90%	86%	81%	76%	70%
3.75	100%	100%	99%	97%	95%	91%	87%	82%	77%	71%	65%
3.50	100%	99%	98%	96%	93%	89%	84%	78%	72%	66%	60%
3.25	100%	99%	97%	94%	90%	85%	79%	73%	67%	60%	54%
3.00	100%	99%	96%	92%	87%	81%	74%	68%	61%	54%	48%
2.75	100%	98%	94%	89%	83%	76%	69%	62%	55%	48%	42%
2.50	99%	96%	91%	85%	78%	70%	62%	55%	48%	42%	36%
2.25	99%	94%	88%	80%	72%	63%	55%	48%	41%	35%	30%
2.00	97%	91%	83%	74%	64%	56%	48%	41%	34%	29%	24%
1.75	95%	86%	76%	66%	56%	48%	40%	33%	28%	23%	19%
1.50	92%	80%	68%	57%	48%	39%	32%	26%	21%	17%	14%
1.25	86%	72%	59%	47%	38%	31%	24%	19%	15%	12%	10%
1.00	78%	61%	47%	37%	29%	22%	17%	14%	11%	8%	6%
0.75	65%	47%	35%	26%	20%	15%	11%	9%	6%	5%	4%
0.50	48%	32%	22%	16%	11%	8%	6%	5%	3%	3%	2%

Source: Moshe Milevsky and the IFID Centre, 2008, based on methodology from Milevsky, M., and Robinson, C., "A Sustainable Spending Rate Without Simulation." *Financial Analysts Journal.* Nov/Dec 2005, 61(6).

Stay with me here. According to the mathematical equations I listed earlier, my retirement alpha is equal to 3 units and my retirement beta is equal to 1.74 units. These are the intermediary ingredients for the main formula.

Finally, I take these two values and look up the retirement sustainability probability from Table 8.3. In the alpha = 3 and beta = 1.74 case, the retirement sustainability probability is approximately 74%. Thus, if I take early retirement today at the age of 40, my odds don't look very good. I will be spending too much, living too long, or simply not earning enough to achieve my sustainability goals.

In contrast, if I were to take early retirement and only spend 2% per year adjusted for inflation, which is $20,000 per $1,000,000 nest egg, the situation would look better. In this case my retirement alpha would be the same 3 units, but my retirement beta would be reduced to 0.70 units. My success ratio would increase to more than 96%. To me, these risk metrics are acceptable, but then again living on $20,000 per year (that is, a 2% spending rate) will be difficult.

Here is another numerical example of the sustainability probability for more realistic portfolio and retirement values. Say you retire with $1,000,000 at the age of 65 when your median remaining lifespan is approximately 19 years. You plan to withdraw $40,000 per year adjusted for your personal inflation rate, which is, thus, a 4% spending rate. Also, assume that your million dollar nest egg is invested in an equity-based mutual fund that is expected to earn an optimistic 7% after (your personal) inflation rate and the estimated volatility rate is 18%. Using values of S=0.04, MRL=19, AM=0.07, and VOL=0.18, according to the equation in Figure 8.3, your retirement alpha is 3.15 units and your retirement beta is 1.16 units. Finally, going down the columns and across the rows, the relevant entry in Table 8.3 is slightly greater than 90%. To me, a 90% sustainability rate is marginally acceptable and is often called the "prudent 4% rule" of retirement spending.

Note that higher values of alpha are good for your retirement, as are lower values of beta. As you move to the lower-right corner, the sustainability numbers decrease, and as you move to the upper-left corner, the sustainability numbers increase. Intuitively, this should make sense if you look carefully at the definitions of alpha and beta. Notice that higher spending rates increase your retirement beta (not good), while higher portfolio returns increase your retirement alpha (good). Also, greater investment volatility reduces your retirement alpha (not good) but also reduces your retirement beta.

Now that you have an intuitive feel for the table, you might wonder where exactly the numbers came from. Or how do you generate your own table with different values of alpha and beta? Actually, this is where the formula I mentioned earlier is used. The tabular values, which are not based on any Monte Carlo simulations, can be obtained by typing the expression *=1-GAMMADIST(beta,alpha,1,TRUE)* within a cell of any Microsoft Excel spreadsheet. In place of the words *alpha* and *beta*, use their actual numerical values calculated using the Figure 8.3 formulas and out pops the precise number from the table.

If you want proof, check out some of the references at the end of the book. And for those of you who remain skeptical that a simple analytic formula offers a shortcut around cumbersome and expensive Monte Carlo simulations of retirement income, I urge you to compare the properly calibrated GAMMADIST results against the output from your favorite financial planning software. Send your thanks to Bill Gates and his team at Excel.

The Effect of Asset Allocation on Sustainability

Clearly, the odds of earning a specific return depend on your asset allocation; that is, on how you divide your capital between stocks, bonds, and other investments.

The technical question I want to investigate using the simple formula I introduced in the previous section is, "How does the asset allocation affect the probability that you will be able to consume $16,000 annually for the rest of your life?"

Let's return to the original example in which a 65-year-old wishes to withdraw 8% per year. Tables 8.4 to 8.6 assume average male and female mortality and provide insight into the effect of asset allocation. Table 8.4 tells us, for example, that if a 65-year-old allocates all of his $200,000 to a short-term bank account or money market fund, earning an annual rate of 1.3% (after inflation), and has zero exposure to the equity markets, there is only a 31.1% chance that this person will be able to consume the desired $16,000. In other words, with a real consumption level of $16,000, there's a 68.9% chance that this person will outlive his money. You will likely agree that this is a very low probability of success. I personally would like to see numbers that are north of 90%, although I could live with numbers as low as 80% if there were some flexibility in my retirement spending budget.

The only difference among Tables 8.4, 8.5, and 8.6 is the age at which the analysis is being conducted. Notice that the older you are when you retire—all else being equal—if you are planning on spending the same amount of money, the sustainability odds are better. This is because, perversely, you have less time ahead of you.

Another byproduct of this sort of analysis is that it sheds light on the affordability, or lack thereof, of early retirement.

Now, what happens if you allocate your assets to funds with somewhat greater volatility but higher long-term growth rates? The fluctuations might hurt in the short term, but what do the overall odds look like when you take account of mortality and investment risk?

TABLE 8.4   What Is the Probability That Spending Is Sustainable? (Age 65; Random Lifespan and Random Returns Under a Fixed Spending Rate)

Allocation to Equity	Needs-to-Wealth Ratio				
	5.0%	**6.0%**	**7.0%**	**8.0%**	**9.0%**
0%	65.0%	52.4%	40.9%	31.1%	23.1%
20%	75.2%	63.9%	52.5%	42.0%	32.9%
40%	80.6%	70.8%	60.5%	50.5%	41.3%
60%	82.6%	74.0%	64.9%	55.8%	47.2%
80%	82.5%	74.7%	66.5%	58.4%	50.5%
100%	81.1%	73.8%	66.3%	58.9%	51.7%

Simulation assumptions: Median remaining lifetime = 18.9;

Equity: expected returns =7%, volatility = 20%; Cash: return =1.3%

Source: Moshe Milevsky and the IFID Centre, 2008.

TABLE 8.5   What Is the Probability That Spending Is Sustainable? (Age 55; Random Lifespan and Random Returns Under a Fixed Spending Rate)

Allocation to Equity	Needs-to-Wealth Ratio				
	5.0%	**6.0%**	**7.0%**	**8.0%**	**9.0%**
0%	43.6%	29.6%	19.1%	11.9%	7.2%
20%	59.7%	44.8%	32.0%	22.0%	14.6%
40%	69.3%	56.0%	43.4%	32.5%	23.6%
60%	73.5%	62.0%	50.8%	40.5%	31.5%
80%	74.4%	64.4%	54.5%	45.2%	36.9%
100%	73.3%	64.3%	55.5%	47.3%	39.8%

Simulation assumptions: Median remaining lifetime = 28 years;

Equity: expected returns =7%, volatility = 20%; Cash: return =1.3%

Source: Moshe Milevsky and the IFID Centre, 2008.

**TABLE 8.6 What Is the Probability That Spending Is Sustainable?
(Age 75; Random Lifespan and Random Returns Under a
Fixed Spending Rate)**

Allocation to	Needs-To-Wealth Ratio				
Equity	5.0%	6.0%	7.0%	8.0%	9.0%
0%	86.4%	79.6%	72.2%	64.6%	57.0%
20%	90.0%	84.4%	78.0%	71.0%	63.9%
40%	91.7%	86.9%	81.2%	75.0%	68.4%
60%	92.2%	87.8%	82.6%	76.9%	70.8%
80%	91.8%	87.5%	82.6%	77.2%	71.5%
100%	90.7%	86.4%	81.5%	76.4%	71.0%

Simulation assumptions: Median remaining lifetime = 10.7 yrs;

Equity: expected returns =7%, volatility = 20%; Cash: return =1.3%

Source: Moshe Milevsky and the IFID Centre, 2008.

As the 65-year-old moves into a more aggressive allocation to equity in Table 8.4, the probability of sustainability, surprisingly, increases. For example, with a 60% allocation to equities and a needs-to-wealth ratio of 8%, the retiree has a sustainability probability of 55.8%. While these odds of success are still fairly low, the higher average long-term rate of return counteracts the effects of the equity investment's short-term volatility, yielding higher "sustainability odds."

A few things should be immediately evident from the three tables. First, retiring at older ages leads to sustainability probabilities that are uniformly higher at all asset allocation levels. For example, under a 100% equity allocation at age 75, the sustainability probability numbers range from 71% to 90.7%, much higher (and much better) than the 51.7% to 81.1% range we see for a 65-year-old in the same situation (in Table 8.4) or the 39.8% to 73.3% for the 55 year-old (in Table 8.5). The reason is quite simple: You are 10 years older and, therefore, have 10 fewer years of consumption ahead of you. The odds of outliving your money, therefore, must be lower.

Another interesting thing to note about Tables 8.4, 8.5, and 8.6 is that the numbers level off at a 60% allocation to equity. In other words, any additional allocation doesn't do much to improve the probability of sustainability. Why is this? Shouldn't higher levels of equity continue to increase the sustainability numbers? Well, the fact is that higher equity allocations will increase the growth rate of your portfolio in the long run. But in the short run, there's always some risk of a bad run of luck. Stated differently, with a 100% allocation to equities, there's a 9% to 15% chance that in the first few years you will experience negative returns. The consequent damage to your capital base is too severe to recover in such a short time horizon. To give a sense of the richness of this formula approach, let's take a look at another set of results. This time, let's consider a 55-year-old, perhaps interested in early retirement and withdrawing only 6%.

From Table 8.5, we can see that a 55-year-old who consumes $12,000 every year from an original nest egg of $200,000 (which represents a 6% needs-to-wealth ratio) has only a 29.6% chance of success or a 70.4% chance of outliving her wealth, if all the money is invested in money market funds. Essentially, with that kind of a low-volatility (and low-return) asset allocation, there is little hope for a successful early retirement. At the other extreme, with a 100% allocation to equities, the odds of success are increased. As you can see, the probability of sustainability increases to 64% or alternatively stated, the chances of outliving wealth is reduced to 36% with a complete allocation to the equity market. Granted, a 36% chance of running short is still rather intimidating, and not tolerable by any means. But the significant reduction from 70% to almost 40% is persuasive, and yields insight into the power of long-term equity growth, despite the associated volatility.

Of course, one could explore countless scenarios for various ages and needs-to-wealth strategies. But in the limited set of presented results, the main relationships emerge.

Finally, Figure 8.4 takes a rather bleak perspective on the issue of retirement probabilities and displays the opposite of the sustainability ratio—the probability of retirement ruin. Yes, an ugly word but I believe it helps shed some additional light on the issue at hand.

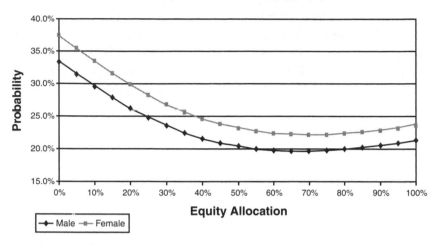

Figure 8.4   Extremes are never good: 70% stocks seem safe.

Source: Moshe Milevsky and the IFID Centre, 2008.

Summary

- There is nothing magical about retirement that should force a more conservative portfolio allocation, especially when you consider longevity risk.

- The method of Monte Carlo simulations is being widely used in the financial services industry to compute and illustrate the impact of various retirement income strategies. Get used to it, and ask your financial or investment advisor to generate a Monte Carlo illustration of your financial future.

- I presented an easy-to-use formula that you can use/apply to test whether your spending plan/rate is sustainable, given the risk/return projections for your retirement portfolio and your current age. Although it is just an approximation, you should strive for sustainability numbers above 90%.

- I think that retirees should have a substantial exposure to equity-based investments, at the very least to beat their personal inflation rate.

- Retirees are obviously still exposed to the risk of a poor sequence of returns, which brings us full circle to the next chapter about annuities.

Endnotes

The article by Bengen (2001) is worth reading because Bengen was one of the first people to conduct Monte Carlo simulations to compute retirement income sustainability. Ho, Milevsky, and Robinson (1994) likely wrote the earliest published paper to combine uncertain lifetime and longevity risk with uncertain investment returns to generate a combined probability of retirement ruin. In my opinion, the article by Markowitz (1991) is the intellectual precursor to retirement income simulations and, more recently, Taleb (2001) provides an excellent critique of the simulations and risk management methodologies, which should remind us to accept all these numbers with the proverbial grain of salt.

9

Annuities Are Personal Pensions

"...Annuities are bad investments because they are expensive, confusing and sold by shady insurance salesmen...."

Myth #9

Annuities are likely one of the most misunderstood and confusing investments in the financial universe. The word *annuity* itself can describe many different instruments, which can be very different from each other. Annuities have received an unbelievable amount of bad press and publicity—some of it justified, some not—yet few people realize that these products are implicitly contained within every single defined benefit (DB) pension plan as well as Social Security. They are the underlying ingredients of retirement plans around the world. Hopefully, this chapter will help clear up some of the confusion and help answer some questions, or at least give you some questions to ask your own financial advisor. But first let me start by telling you an interesting story and review some history of my limited role and involvement in the annuity industry's bad publicity.

In the mid-1990s, I conducted and subsequently published a widely cited research study, together with a risk analyst from Goldman Sachs, on the nature and magnitude of fees and expenses charged within variable annuities (VA). The basic chassis of a generic variable annuity is quite similar to a mutual fund but it is classified as an insurance product because of various explicit and implicit insurance guarantees. Hence, annuities also benefit from a more favorable tax treatment by having all investment gains within the policy sheltered from taxes until the policy is surrendered. I'll get to the details of my research study a little bit later in the chapter, but the bottom line is that my early verdict wasn't very kind to VAs. They didn't make much sense to me.

In general, an annuity is best viewed as a process as opposed to just a product. Think of it as having a life cycle of its own that starts at birth, grows over time, and finally matures. The early part of the process consists of a pay-in stage and is illustrated in Figure 9.1. Here the policyholder or investor contributes money (either in one lump sum or over time) with the funds allocated among a number of subaccounts that move up and down in value over time. The goal of this process, like any other investment, is to grow the account by receiving dividends, capital gains, and interest.

The Annuity Life Cycle

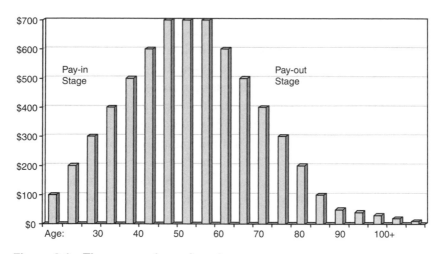

Figure 9.1   The personal pension plan.

Source: Moshe Milevsky and the IFID Centre, 2008.

This growth phase will come to an end in one of three different ways, summarized in Figure 9.2. The policyholder may do one of the following:

- Decide to surrender (also known as lapse) the policy by withdrawing the entire sum of money

- Die, which would result in a guaranteed minimum death benefit (GMDB) to a beneficiary
- Opt to receive slow and periodic income payments, which is the pay-out stage depicted in Figure 9.1. The slow and periodic income payments can be guaranteed for life, for a fixed period of time, or until the money runs out.

So, these are basically the three exit strategies (if you can call dying a strategy) for terminating an annuity policy, as shown in Figure 9.2. Each of these exit points is important in their own right, because there might be guarantees associated with each of these triggering events. And, obviously, the more guarantees that are included within the basic annuity structure, the more it might make sense to include them in your investment portfolio. If you are considering one of these, whether inside a 401(k) or IRA, or outside of a tax shelter, make sure you understand exactly how these events will impact the value of your account and the amount of money you can withdraw.

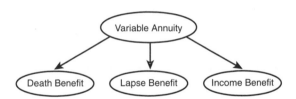

Figure 9.2   Three ways out....

Source: Moshe Milevsky and the IFID Centre, 2008.

Now let me get back to my statistical study of the late 1990s. At the time we conducted our research, most VA policies were only offering a basic guaranteed return-of-premium (RoP) death benefit, which meant that at the market's worst you got your money back, and only if you died. These guaranteed minimum death benefits, or GMDBs as they are abbreviated, were the only relevant guaranteed features that distinguished VA policies from their mutual fund cousins.

Yes, during the mid-1990s some insurance companies started offering variable annuities with more lucrative minimum investment returns or maximum anniversary guarantees. These enhanced GMDBs promised that in the event of death, beneficiaries would be guaranteed at least the premium deposit, grown by up to 7% per annum, or a death benefit equal to the best historical anniversary value. But then again, you had to die to get these benefits and many policies were surrendered and lapsed well before the policyholder ever died. More importantly, at the time of our analysis the bulk of VA assets—and especially the policies inside tax-sheltered qualified plans such as 401(k) or IRA accounts—only offered a plain vanilla (RoP) GMDB.

To conduct the study, we examined a comprehensive database that Morningstar graciously provided to us, which at the time included over 400 VA policies and 7,000 investment subaccounts. That was then. Now, there are over 1,400 different policies and a mind-numbing 66,000 different investment subaccounts to choose from. (Talk about inflation for retirees!) We compared the pure insurance charges, called the mortality and expense (M&E) fee—which ranged from 7 to more than 140 basis points (or 0.07% to 1.40%) per annum—to theoretical model values, which approximated the costs of replicating these guarantees in the capital markets. Think of it as comparing retail prices to wholesale prices for a pair of shoes, to calculate the markup.

This might sound like an odd type of project to do as a hobby in your spare time, but it was pure intellectual curiosity that motivated us to investigate whether consumers were getting their money's worth on the guarantees offered within variable annuities.

Nowadays, the question of whether the costs and fees charged within a variable annuity contract are "too high" or "too low" or "just about right" relative to some baseline economic valuation model, is not just a theoretical exercise in abstract pricing theory. This topic is relevant to more than just the cost-conscious investors or consumer advocates who want to make sure they are getting fair value for their money. In fact, no less authority than the U.S. Department of Labor has recently issued regulations that pertain to the fiduciary responsibilities of trustees in defined contribution (DC) pension plans. The DOL regulates these plans and has a critical voice in deciding what investments should be allowed into DC plans. Their recent regulations explicitly mention the importance and centrality of the costs and fees of annuities within DC plans. According to the DOL, those who are tasked with the responsibility of selecting annuities as a form of accumulation or distribution within a DC plan "...*must* consider the costs of an annuity contract in relation to the benefits and administrative services provided."

As far as the original study was concerned, the embedded guarantees promised at death were quite similar to equity put options, which are contracts that grant the holder a right but not an obligation to sell an underlying portfolio at a fixed price on a given date. Put options are traded on financial exchanges all over the world and have readily available market prices. In the VA case, instead of the option maturing at a fixed date such as three weeks, months, or years in the future, the maturity date of the option was random; namely a date of death. Partially tongue in cheek, we called these securities, Titanic options.

Alas, our main research conclusion was that, if the extra added insurance fee was only meant to cover true risk, the typical VA policyholder was being grossly overcharged for the protection and peace of mind. We found that the basic RoP guarantee (that is, you get your money back at death) was worth no more than 5 to 10 basis points (or 0.05% to 0.10%) of assets per annum. Now, this obviously depended on the exact age of the policyholder, because older investors are more likely to die and hence cash in on the guarantee. Table 9.1 displays the theoretical model values of the death benefit guarantees for policy holders age 30 through 65.

TABLE 9.1   Capital Market Cost of a GMDB: RoP Guarantee

Age	Female	Male
30	0.3 b.p.	0.4 b.p.
40	0.8 b.p.	1.3 b.p.
50	2.0 b.p.	3.5 b.p.
60	5.0 b.p.	8.7 b.p.
65	7.6 b.p.	13.0 b.p.

b.p. = basis point

Assumptions: Equity: expected returns = 6%, volatility = 20%

Source: Moshe Milevsky and the IFID Centre, 2008.

For example, consider a 60-year-old female who invests her nest egg of $100,000 among various equity mutual funds and wants to purchase a guarantee that would return the entire initial $100,000 sum to her beneficiary upon her death. According to Table 9.1, she would need to pay 5.0 basis points (which is 0.05%) of her account value per year. Assume for a moment that the account grows to $110,000 by the end of the first year and the guarantee fee is charged at the end of each year. This means that she would pay 0.05%*$110,000= $55 for this protection for the first year.

I don't want to get caught up in the mathematical details here, but these are model values, since it is very difficult to purchase capital market guarantees with maturities that are 40 to 50 years into the future. Yet, the mathematical models tell us that they are worth no more than a few basis points because they can theoretically be replicated for this cost. In plain English, we were arguing that people should just get some token life insurance. It will be cheaper.

Once again, an RoP guarantee essentially promises that at death you will get no less than your money back. That is the lower bound or worst-case scenario. There are some products and companies that offer a better worst-case scenario return, often called death benefits with look-back or ratchet guarantees, and those are worth a bit more, as illustrated in Table 9.2. The word "ratchet" refers to the fact that every time the account value within the variable annuity moves up (or ratchets) to a higher level, the death benefit is reset.

TABLE 9.2   Capital Market Cost of a GMDB:
Look-Back (Ratchet) Guarantee

Age	Female	Male
30	15.1 b.p.	25.0 b.p.
40	18.9 b.p.	31.6 b.p.
50	24.6 b.p.	41.8 b.p.
60	32.8 b.p.	56.4 b.p.
65	36.1 b.p.	62.5 b.p.

b.p. = basis point

Assumptions: Equity: expected returns = 6%, volatility = 20%

Source: Moshe Milevsky and the IFID Centre, 2008.

I don't want to get lost in the details of these various life insurance guarantees, but for the most part, their "replicating costs" or "hedging costs" are quite low. Stated differently, Tables 9.1 and 9.2 give a rough sense of the wholesale cost the insurance company would have to pay to insure themselves against the same risks they are insuring you against. Otherwise described as the amounts it would cost the insurance company that is offering the guarantee to hedge its exposure to this risk. Even the more lucrative (although at that time rare) death benefits guarantees that promised more than just your original investment were worth no more than 60 basis points (or 0.60%) at most. The high estimate applied only if you were male, old enough to be close to death, risk tolerant enough to invest aggressively, and persistent enough not to surrender (also known in the tax jargon as an IRC section 1035 exchange) your policy prior to death.

In addition to these results, our research study reported on a number of other peculiarities in the VA market. As you can see from the tables, we found that older (unhealthy) males who invested more aggressively were receiving a guarantee that was much more valuable to them relative to younger (healthy) females who invested conservatively. This was because the odds of dying during a bear market, which was the only way the insurance guarantee would pay off, were much higher for the former group compared to the latter. Yet both groups were paying the exact same level of insurance fees. It was akin to traditional life insurance that is sold to young and old, healthy and sick, for exactly the same premium. Likewise, the extra insurance fees were being charged independently of the actual asset allocation of the underlying subaccounts, even though the chances of a bond fund or money market fund being underwater at a random time of death was close to zero. We couldn't help but wonder: Why weren't subaccount risk fees being prorated by the true risk? Anyway, none of this made much sense to us at the time, especially given our training as financial economists where markets and prices are supposed to reflect costs and benefits. So, we threw our hands up and declared, "Why would anyone buy this?"

These findings were eventually published in the prestigious *Journal of Risk and Insurance* in 2001 and subsequently quoted in publications ranging from *The Wall Street Journal* and *Newsweek* to

Reader's Digest. Our findings were seized upon by investor advocates, financial commentators, regulators, and plaintiff lawyers as evidence that variable annuities were overpriced, oversold, and unsuitable. At the time, I was quite surprised at the attention this report garnered, because the article was full of equations and regressions, which normally don't travel beyond the ivory tower.

In fact, I actually ended up taking the witness stand in a number of related lawsuits and regulatory actions to opine that a promise of getting your money back when you die was "kind of pointless" and at the very least could be replicated using cheaper forms of life insurance.

Indeed, I still stand behind those results, even if it means that I occasionally come face-to-face with disgruntled insurance industry executives who believe that our results were misguided. Remember, I never said that variable annuities were evil, dangerous, or unsuitable. Our basic position was that for many investors, a similar financial outcome could be achieved at a lower cost.

Times and Products Are Changing

However, in the last few years that I have been observing this industry, I am seeing a titanic shift in the way VA policies are being designed, priced, and marketed to the public. Namely, right now a much greater focus is being placed on the "pay-out" stage of the annuity lifecycle and the concept of annuitization. Either way, it is now time for me to update my official position on these instruments. But first things first, let's get a better understanding of the pay-out phase and how exactly a pension annuity really works.

What Exactly Is Annuitization?

Traditionally, when an annuity policyholder ends the pay-in phase by electing to receive a guaranteed income benefit, he is said to annuitize the account or to purchase an immediate or pay-out annuity. This "A" word strikes fear into the hearts and wallets of investors because it involves irreversibly handing over a lump sum of money—to an insurance company, no less. In exchange for the lump sum, the company promises to slowly return this money until the day of the retiree's death. This irreversibility also creates the concern that the value of the account is lost to the family and loved ones because in the event of death, and if no guarantee period is selected, the insurance company retains any remaining unpaid portion.

Given the permanence of this action, this transaction might rightfully feel like financial suicide to many retirees. Ironically, as I mentioned earlier in the chapter, the loathed process of annuitization is at the core of defined benefit (DB) pensions—a steady generator of retirement income, which is cherished by retired civil servants around the world. In fact, the income from Social Security is also based on a type of annuitization process. You can't securitize, cash in, or monetize your income stream, although it definitely lasts for the rest of your life. And, aside from providing longevity insurance, annuitization offers a substantial benefit to the retiree in the form of mortality credits. I'll explain more about this in a minute.

So which one is it then? Is annuitization odious or perhaps is it the foundation of a well-balanced retirement income plan and hedging strategy? In an attempt to address the fog of confusion surrounding the financial benefits of annuities, allow me to digress a bit and provide a closer look at the pros and the cons. Indeed, if you are going to accept annuitization as a partial solution for your retirement income, then you should understand the mechanics of how they work. And, if you plan to bypass them as viable solutions, then it makes sense to talk intelligently about their shortcomings.

The Pros of Annuitization

As I mentioned, an immediate annuity provides lifetime income that cannot be outlived, making it an invaluable hedging tool against longevity risk, which I discussed in past chapters. Recall, this is the risk of unexpected improvement in mortality and/or that a retiree lives far beyond any average life expectancy. Think of it as the equivalent of systematic/economic risk versus individual risk, which I explained in Chapter 3, "Diversification over Space and Time."

Immediate annuities thus provide a mechanism for pooling, sharing, and hedging longevity risk over a large population, which leads to a higher yield for annuitants. Finally, they provide stable and predictable income that is not subject to the vagaries of the stock market. It's a fixed-income bond product together with a longevity coupon "kicker."

To get a better understanding on how this works, Table 9.3 provides some real-world data and displays sample quotes for single premium immediate annuities (SPIAs as they are often abbreviated) in late 2007. Each column contains the best five quotes for the given starting age and gender. These numbers are provided by a company called CANNEX Financial Exchanges, which is attempting to provide the equivalent of a stock exchange quoting system for retirement income products.

TABLE 9.3   What Does $100,000 Buy You?
Monthly Income for Life

Company	65-Year-Old Male		65-Year-Old Female	
	No PC	10-Yr PC	No PC	10-Yr PC
A	$711	$681	$658	$641
B	$695	$668	$650	$635
C	$689	$659	$639	$623
D	$681	$656	$633	$618
E	$678	$655	$629	$613

Source: CANNEX Financial Exchanges, November 2007.

Here is how to read the numbers in Table 9.3. For example, if a 65-year-old female invests or allocates $100,000 into a SPIA, then the upper range for lifetime income that she will receive is $629 to $658 per month, depending on which insurance carrier is selected. Note that this income stream will completely cease upon death. If she dies ten, five, or even one year into the annuitization period, everything is lost. Naturally, many people select a guarantee period for their SPIA, at the expense of a slightly lower income stream. For example, as shown in the same table, if the 65-year-old female selects a 10-year payment certain (PC, as they are often called), the upper income range is now lower; the best offer is $641 per month and the lowest offer is $613. A 65-year-old male gets slightly more. His numbers range from $655 to $681 if he selects a 10-year period certain and $678 to $711 if he does not.

On a slightly more technical level, if you divide the annual income generated by the SPIA, by the initial premium of $100,000, you arrive at the important annuity yield. For example, using payouts from Table 9.3 at age 65, with zero years of certain payments, the yield ranges from 8.14% (=678*12/100,000) to 8.53% for males and 7.55% to 7.90% for females.

Indeed, these annuity yields have been steadily declining over the last few decades as a result of both lower long-term interest rates as well as increasing longevity.

Figure 9.3 illustrates the monthly evolution of the annuity yield over the last few years. I have plotted the best/worst annuity yields, for both males and females, offered by insurance companies in the U.S., as well as the yield on a 10-year government bond.

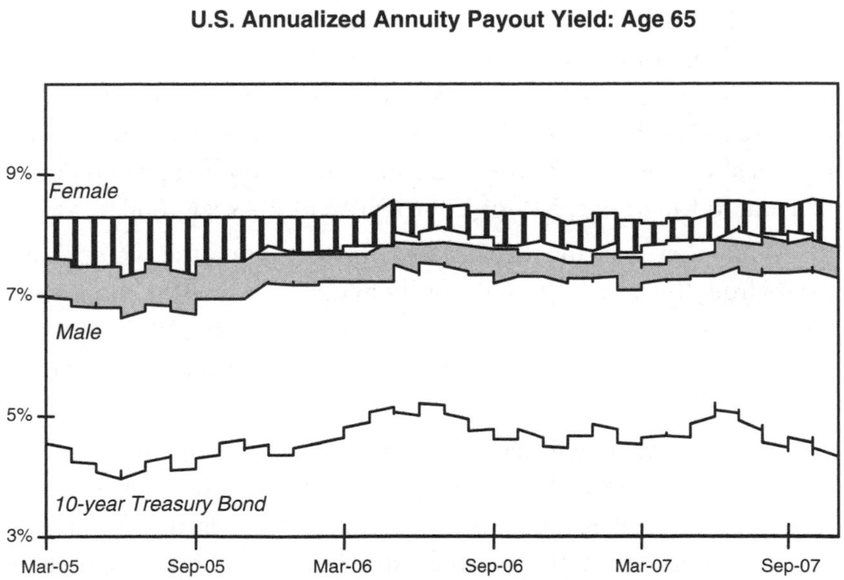

U.S. Annualized Annuity Payout Yield: Age 65

Figure 9.3   Immediate annuities always yield more than bonds.

Source: CANNEX Financial Exchanges, November 2007; IFID Centre calculations.

A number of important insights can be gleaned from this chart. First, notice that the yield, which once again is the annualized income stream divided by the initial premium, is much greater than the yield on a government bond. The reason for this is because your income is an integrated blend of three distinct cash flows: First, you are getting a type of interest coupon on your money; second, you are getting a portion of your premium back, and third—the main benefit derived from the annuity—you are getting some of other people's money.

What do I mean by "other people's money"? This is what I earlier referred to as mortality credits, and here is a simple tale that can illustrate this concept, as well as the benefits of annuitization and longevity insurance.

Yet Another Digression—The Tontine

Imagine a group of five healthy 95-year-old females, all coincidentally celebrating their 95th birthday on the same day. To bring some excitement to the party, they decide to engage in an odd gamble. Each of the five women agrees to contribute $100 to a pool. The funds will be frozen for a year, they decide. "Whoever survives to the end of the year gets to split the $500; whoever doesn't make it, forfeits the money." This type of arrangement is known as a tontine, and is named after Lorenzo Tonti, an Italian banker who first promoted the concept to King Louis XIV of France around the year 1650.

While they wait for the next year to determine the winners and losers from the tontine, the five of them decide to put the money in a local bank's one-year certificate of deposit (CD) paying 5% interest for the year. The CD will mature at $525 at year end, just in time for their 96th birthday.

So what exactly will happen next year? Who will survive? How much will they get? Well, according to statistics compiled by actuaries at the U.S. Social Security administration, there is roughly a 20% chance that any given 95-year-old will die during the next year. This, in turn, implies an 80% chance of survival for any one of them. These odds imply that we expect four out of five women to survive and make it to their 96th birthday to split the $525 pot at year-end.

Note that each survivor will get $131.25 as her total return on the original investment of $100. The 31.25% investment return contains 5% of the bank's money and a healthy 26.25% of something we call "mortality credits." These credits represent the capital and interest "lost" by the deceased and "gained" by the survivors.

The catch, of course, is that the average nonsurvivor forfeited her claim to the funds. And while the beneficiaries of the nonsurvivor might be frustrated with the outcome, the survivors get a superior investment return. Personally, I find no other financial product that guarantees such high rates of return, conditional on survival.

More importantly, they *all* get to manage their lifetime income risk in advance, without having to worry about what the future will bring. This is the essence of the benefit from immediate annuities.

In fact, this story can be taken one step further. What if the group decided to invest the $500 in the stock market, or some risky NAS-DAQ high-tech fund, for the next year? Moreover, what happens if this fund or subaccount collapses in value during the next year and falls 20% in value to $400? How much will the surviving members lose? Well, if you are thinking "nothing," that is absolutely the correct answer. They divide the $400 among the surviving four and get their original $100 back.

Such is the power of mortality credits. They subsidize losses on the downside and enhance gains on the upside. In fact, I would go so far as to say that once you wrap true longevity insurance around a diversified portfolio, the annuitant can actually afford and tolerate more financial risk.

Of course, real live annuity contracts do not work in the way described previously. The group's "tontine" contract is renewable each year and the surviving 96-year-olds have the option to take their mortality credits and go home. In practice, annuity contracts are for life and these credits are spread and amortized over many years of retirement. The annuitant receives a constant periodic check that blends all of these varying components. But the basic insurance economics underlying the contract are exactly as described earlier.

While this life-roulette game would not yield such high returns at younger ages—and one might be better off managing the money oneself with a systematic withdrawal plan—by the mid-'80s beating the implied return offered by immediate annuities becomes virtually impossible. To put it crudely, too many people are dying.

Back to Real-World Immediate Annuities

Notice also another subtle but interesting fact in Figure 9.3. The spread between the highest/lowest quotes, that is, what the most competitive versus least competitive insurance company is offering, appears to be shrinking over time. In other words, the gains from shopping or the dispersion between companies is on the decline.

My personal theory is that the declining spread between the highest and lowest quotes reflects a market that is becoming more commoditized and more competitive. And, although insurance companies might not welcome this trend, the end user can only benefit. In fact, the availability of the Internet—and the CANNEX Financial Exchange, which provides a transparent platform for users to see quotes in real time—helps accelerate this trend.

The Cons of Annuitization

A number of legitimate criticisms are often leveled against SPIAs and other annuitization-based products. I have already mentioned one of the major concerns, and that is the almost complete irreversibility of the decision after the policy has been funded and the product is acquired. Unlike almost any other financial instrument, like a stock, bond, or mutual fund, one cannot redeem, cash in, or even sell a SPIA in the secondary market. In many cases you completely cede any estate value when you annuitize.

To be honest, although this irreversibility is frustrating, it is perfectly understandable and justifiable. Imagine what would happen if individuals who are in poor health, or are perhaps even on their death bed, were allowed to "return" their SPIA certificate to the insurance company and then ask for a refund against all the payments they had not yet received. Obviously, everyone would do this and the insurance companies would completely lose their ability to diversify longevity risk across a large pool of annuitants. This is another example of adverse selection, which I discussed in Chapter 2, "Insurance Is a Hedge for Human Capital," and is one of the great justifiable fears for insurance actuaries. Remember, the reason you are getting the yield above and beyond what is available in the fixed-income bond market is because the insurance company can internally subsidize longevity.

Some companies have responded to the lack of liquidity concern by offering cleverly engineered SPIAs that provide partial-liquidity, refunds, and death benefits. And although these solutions might alleviate retirees' concerns about annuitization, they come at the expense of the aforementioned longevity credits.

Second, inflation is a concern, and specifically how it impacts retirement income, a topic I tackled in Chapter 5, "Personal Inflation and the Retirement Cost of Living." Remember that most currently sold SPIA products provide nominal payments that decay in real terms over time. The purchasing power of that income may decline by more than 60% by the time you are halfway through your retirement. Of course, you can purchase inflation-linked or cost of living adjusted (COLA) life annuities, but the price you pay is greatly reduced upfront payments.

A third quite legitimate concern is credit risk—the risk that the insurance company is unable to meet its payment obligations to the annuitant sometime in the future. Right now the best-rated insurance company in the U.S. offering SPIA products has a rating of Aa1 according to Moody's Investor Services, while the lowest in our sample was rated A1. While these ratings are at the upper-end of Moody's scale, many buyers are concerned about the possibility of downgrades and eventual defaults over long horizons. The reassurance that is offered to these buyers is that insurance company defaults are rare and that state guaranteed funds do exist to protect policyholders up to a limit. However one easy solution would be to diversify across companies and, hence, reduce some risk that way.

In sum, immediate annuities provide a very unique and peculiar kind of insurance. It is virtually the only insurance policy that people acquire during the course of their life but actually hope to use! While we are all willing to pay for home insurance, disability insurance, or car insurance, we never actually want to exercise or use the policy.

After all, who wants their house to burn down, leg to break, or car to crash? Yet, the "insurable event" underlying pension annuities is living a long and prosperous life.

Back to My Research on Variable Annuities

So, after spending quite a bit of time pouring over some of the more recent designs of variable annuities as well as talking to actuaries, regulators, and advisors, I'm not even sure these instruments and riders deserve the old (maligned) variable annuity name.

Regardless of what you want to call these increasingly heterogeneous products, it seems the relative value pendulum has swung in the opposite direction. I can no longer claim that you are being overcharged for their guarantees or that you can achieve similar goals at a lower cost.

Nowadays, VA policies are not being manufactured as an investment to die for but as an investment to live for because they are increasingly focused on generating a lifetime of income that is guaranteed. They certainly are not being marketed as a primary tax shelter. Increasingly cheaper term life insurance and lower capital gains tax rates have rightfully taken the wind out of those sails. Currently the main story is about protection against the sequence of returns risk, which I discussed in Chapter 6, "Sequence of Investment Returns," and a sustainable retirement income that will last a lifetime and beyond, without the scary irreversibility of annuitization. Alas, the variable annuity has finally returned to its roots I tried to explain earlier. It is providing longevity insurance; and it would be very difficult and expensive to create a "living benefit" in a do-it-yourself manner.

Indeed, when you take into account the new living benefit riders being attached to variable annuities, such as Guaranteed Minimum Withdrawal Benefits (GMWBs), Guaranteed Minimum Accumulation Benefits (GMABs), and Guaranteed Minimum Income Benefits (GMIBs), these "FinSurance" products are creating a different type of protection. The characteristics of these elected riders are summarized in Table 9.4 and despite the odd sounding acronyms, all of them include equity put options on the capital market. They protect the owner in the event that something goes awfully wrong during the early part of their retirement or when they start generating income. And after the market meltdown earlier this decade, the sequence of returns risk might not be as remote as during the euphoria of the late '90s. Indeed, markets don't have to go down and stay down to ruin your retirement. All you need is a bear market at the wrong time, and the sustainability of your income can be cut in half.

TABLE 9.4   The Increasing Galaxy of Annuity Riders

What Is It Called?	Clunky Acronym	What Exactly Does It Do?
Income Benefit	*GMIB Guaranteed Minimum Income Benefit*	Provides the ability to convert the "best" or "most favorable" policy value into lifetime income at a guaranteed rate by annuitizing
Withdrawal Benefit	*GMWB fL Guaranteed Minimum Withdrawal Benefit (for Life)*	Allows for a systematic withdrawal plan that guarantees a minimal income for a fixed period of time (for example, 10 to 25 years) or in some case, for life
Accumulation Benefit	*GMAB Guaranteed Minimum Accumulation Benefit*	Guarantees to return "at least" your entire original investment back, if not more, at some predetermined horizon (for example, 10 years) or age
Longevity Benefit	*ALDA Advanced Life Delayed Annuity*	Provides lifetime income that starts at advanced ages (for example, 85) in exchange for a small insurance premium that you pay upfront or over time

Source: Moshe Milevsky and the IFID Centre, 2008.

Are the Fees (Still) Too High?

This leads me to my main point, which is that I'm now getting the impression that the latest guarantees and riders offered with variable annuities are actually worth much more than what some insurance companies are charging in pure insurance fees.

Yes, this sounds like an odd thing to say given the position of my earlier study. But, when I analyze the extra rider fees charged in the name of these living benefit guarantees, I can't help but wonder why Wall Street's investment bankers charge so much more for the same type of derivative security (essentially long-term put options) when they are purchased on a stand-alone basis. To review once more, put options are contracts that offer the purchaser a right but not the obligation to sell an asset at a predetermined "strike" price. And when I obtained some pricey quotes for buying stand-alone put options to protect a hypothetical retiree's lifetime income, I first thought it was the derivatives dealers and option market makers that were overcharging. To illustrate these high costs, in Table 9.5 I include the approximate cost of protecting $500,000 invested in a hypothetical fund (that exactly tracks the performance of the SP500) for one month, one year, and two years. Based on the cost of a one-month put option, it would cost approximately 2.73% or $13,650!

TABLE 9.5   Cost of Protection in Capital Markets (SP500 Spot Price =$1,440)

Option Expiration	Upfront Cost	Annualized Cost
1 Month	2.73%	—
1 Year	9.08%	908 b.p.
2 Years	11.97%	599 b.p.

Source: Chicago Board Options Exchange put price quotes as of 11/22/07and IFID Centre calculations; costs are an upper bound.

But, after some careful analysis, the same mathematical models that told us a decade ago that basic death benefit guarantees were overpriced were now telling us that many living benefits, for the most part, were underpriced.

As an example, I recently conducted a follow-up study with a colleague of mine at York University demonstrating that the basic GMWB rider, which charges an extra 30 to 50 b.p. in practice, might actually cost between 75 and 160 b.p. to hedge in the capital markets. And, that number does not even include any insurance company profit margins, commissions, and transaction costs. Indeed, the options exchange, which is the only other place an investor can buy similar investment crash protection, often charges five to ten times that number during periods of market stress (volatility).

As I mentioned earlier, in addition to offering a hedge against the sequence of returns in retirement, innovative riders such as the GMWB for life and GMIB can implicitly serve as longevity insurance. This represents a solution for those retirees who are not comfortable with the irreversibility of annuitization and for those affected by the gradual "extinction" of defined benefit pension plans. Of course, this represents a challenge to the insurance companies offering the guarantee given that they are assuming more longevity risk—a risk that most defined benefit pension plans are running away from in droves.

In sum, more than two trillion dollars is sitting in VA policies. Many are still old-style VA policies whose guarantees are (still) worth no more than a few basis points of assets. But the rest of this money is allocated to VA policies with valuable living benefit options that might end up presenting a challenge to their issuers for many years to come. Note that I am not necessarily advocating that insurance companies act in tandem to increase the fees on these riders, and I don't think the U.S. Justice Department would take lightly to such a suggestion either. Rather, that in this living benefits arms race, it will become more important than ever before for these issuers to implement adequate hedging strategies in the case that interest rates decline or longevity increases far more than expected. This will directly impact their ability to honor their promises and guarantees down the road. One thing is for sure: This type of insurance is worthwhile.

At the absolute least, take a close and careful look at Figure 9.4 so that you can identify the type of annuity you are considering. There is an entire universe of products and strategies with the word *annuity* in the title. Some of them have very little to do with the annuity's longevity insurance concept I described previously.

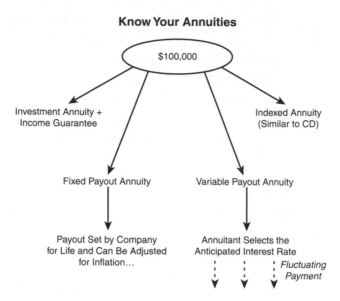

Figure 9.4   All use the word annuity, but are very different.

Source: Moshe Milevsky and the IFID Centre, 2008.

Summary

- Annuities have been around for thousands of years and are the foundation of defined benefit (DB) pension plans as well as the U.S. Social Security system. There is nothing inherently wrong or problematic with annuities. They are risk management instruments, and you ignore them at your own risk.

- Think of a variable annuity as a mutual fund with a selection of different investment options, together with a number of implicit and explicit guarantees.

- Some of these guarantees are quite valuable and some are not as valuable. For the most part and, in general, the new generation of guaranteed living income benefits (abbreviated GLiBs) are very different compared to the old-style death-benefit guarantees. These GLiBs will provide fair value to the consumer and, therefore, make more sense to me as appropriate for funding one's retirement.

Endnotes

This chapter draws heavily from and is inspired by the original research that I published with Steven Posner in the *Journal of Risk and Insurance* (2001) and the follow-up research I published with Thomas Salisbury in *Insurance: Mathematics and Economics* (2006). Please see Milevsky (2006) for additional background and references.

10 ———

Product Allocation Is the New Asset Allocation

"Asset allocation explains 95% of investment performance."

Myth #10

In the early years of our financial life, as we are busily working and converting our human capital into financial capital, the single most important piece of economic wisdom that one should strive to implement is the concept of diversification. Proper diversification is usually practiced by making sure that our financial capital is allocated across many diverse and uncorrelated asset classes, which hopefully do not share the same risk factors as our human capital. Indeed, asset allocation—whether it is across stocks and bonds, value and growth, small cap and large cap—is the cornerstone of diversification. The two ideas go hand in hand.

However, as we get closer to retirement, I believe that asset allocation takes on a more limited role, compared to the much more important and critical decision of a suitable product allocation. By the term product allocation, I mean the decision of how much of your retirement income should come from conventional financial instruments, such as mutual funds or exchange traded funds, and how much should be generated by pension-like products, such as life annuities, variable annuities, and other guaranteed insurance products. In this chapter, I discuss and present one possible approach to determining a suitable Product Allocation for Retirement Income, which is abbreviated by the acronym PrARI®.[1]

Introduction to Product Allocation

As I have argued and demonstrated in previous chapters, as individuals transition from wealth accumulation (converting their human capital) to income generation (spending their financial capital), they face unique and different risks that simply do not arise in the years prior to retirement. As a brief refresher, I review these risks before I introduce my main thesis regarding optimal product allocation for retirement income.

Longevity Risk

The National Center of Health Statistics reports that American life expectancy at birth has increased by about 15 years in the last 50 years alone. It is now estimated to be 75.2 years for males and 80.4 years for females. Of course, averages alone don't tell the entire story because when we actually reach our retirement years, the chances of surviving for another 20 to 30 years are quite substantial. I covered this all in great length in Chapter 7, "Longevity Is a Blessing and a Risk."

For instance a typical 65-year-old male has nearly a 46% chance of surviving another 20 years. A female's chances are even greater. One of every two 65-year-olds females alive today is estimated to survive to the age 85. Perhaps the most compelling of longevity statistics are the probabilities of survival for at least one member of a couple. For example, the chance that at least one member of a couple (where both are 65-years-old) survives to age 85 is 76%; the probability that one spouse or even both are alive at age 90 are one in two.

While individual lifestyle factors, behavioral habits, and family history will obviously impact any survival estimates, my main point is to remind the reader that human lifespan is random and a retirement strategy must—more so than ever before—account for this longevity risk.

Inflation Risk

The U.S. Federal Reserve is dedicated to ensuring that macroeconomic inflation is kept at acceptable levels. They do this by fine-tuning monetary policy so that the change in the Consumer Price

Index (CPI), and other aggregate measures of inflation that they track, are kept within a certain range. However, the U.S. Federal Reserve doesn't target and will never accept a zero percent inflation rate target. Thus, what many retirees fail to realize is that even a very low inflation rate can have a detrimental effect on their purchasing power several years into retirement.

If you recall from Chapter 5, "Personal Inflation and the Retirement Cost of Living," even an inflation rate as low as 2% can reduce the purchasing power of $1,000 by more than a third after 20 years of erosion. And, after 35 years, the initial $1,000 is only worth half of its original value in real terms under the same 2% inflation rate.

The mathematics of purchasing power erosion is even more pronounced for retirees. Aside from the CPI, by now you should be aware that the U.S. Bureau of Labor Statistics recently inaugurated a new unique inflation index for the elderly, which they call CPI-E. The need for this new index arises because as we age, our spending habits change. Any inflation index, after all, is a reflection of a given basket of goods, and this new index aims to capture retirees' spending patterns. It turns out that the CPI-E has actually outpaced the broad population CPI by 0.5% to 1% per year throughout much of the past 25 years. What this all means is that inflation is different and is higher for retirees.

Sequence of Returns

In Chapter 6, "Sequence of Investment Returns," I demonstrated how in the years just before and just after retirement, also known as the fragile risk zone, a retiree's nest egg is most sensitive to losses from poor market returns. This is the point at which the greatest amount of money is at stake. Thus, if investment returns are sequenced so that negative returns are earned early on in retirement, the sustainability of the spending strategy may be threatened. Of course, one cannot control the timing of an inevitable bear market, just as we have no control over the precise length and cost of our lifespan or the rate of inflation throughout our retirement.

Thus—and this is one of my main points that motivate the need for a product allocation strategy—rather than trying to predict the outcomes of any of these random events, I believe one should *insure against adverse outcomes* using a product allocation strategy. In a sense the objective is to hedge against these retirement risks in the context of one's retirement goals.

Given the growing importance of retirement risk management, it is not surprising that the financial services industry is continuously expanding its repertoire of insurance and investment products and their embedded features. The resulting challenge is determining which of these products should be recommended for allocating a client's wealth and in what proportions.

As a starting point, I would argue that there are three principal financial and insurance categories that should be considered for a comprehensive product allocation strategy.

First, the systematic withdrawal plan (or SWiP) is a strategy in which money is systematically withdrawn from a fund allocated among various investments to generate a retirement income. This process continues until the account value hits zero, or until the end of the retiree's life cycle.

Second, the latest generation of variable annuities offers the option to elect a number of riders or features with embedded guarantees that address retirement risks. The growing list of acronyms includes the GMAB (guaranteed minimum accumulation benefit), GMWB (guaranteed minimum withdrawal benefit) and GMIB (guaranteed minimum income benefit). These features and their associated promises were summarized in Table 9.4. The GMWB and the GMIB are of particular interest for the discussion of retirement income, and going forward I refer to them as guaranteed living benefits or GLiBs.

Finally, this brings us back to lifetime pay-out income annuities (LPIAs), also known as single premium immediate annuities (SPIAs) or fixed immediate annuities (FIAs). The primary risk-management benefit of this product is that it provides the buyer with longevity insurance. The embedded longevity insurance protects the annuitants against outliving their life expectancy. That is what you are insuring against by acquiring a LPIA, and to a certain extent, a guaranteed living income benefit (GLiB). Moreover, the longevity insurance is even more valuable when the LPIA is purchased early in life (for example, prior to age 50) with payments that commence late in life (for example, after age 80). In fact, the greater the gap between the purchase date and the commencement date, all else being equal, the greater are the embedded mortality credits, which is a term actuaries use to describe pure longevity insurance. This type of plan is often referred to as an ALDA or an advanced life delayed annuity and is also included in Table 9.4.

Guaranteed living income benefits (GLiBs) on the other hand, by virtue of the fact that they are not pure LPIA products, like the ones described previously, don't contain as much longevity insurance. They contain some, because in some cases they do promise payments for life; but they also provide another form of insurance against a poor sequence of returns. This is in addition to giving you access to a diversified variety of investment funds, like stocks, bonds, and other conventional securities. Because of its unique combination of insurance against a collection of risks, I consider it to be its own risk management product and worthy of its own allocation.

Before determining which of these three categories are appropriate for a particular retiree and in what combination, it is important to gauge their relative strengths and shortfalls.

In Figure 10.1, I assign a relative numerical score to each of the three products based on its effectiveness at hedging the three retirement risks and addressing retirement goals. Collectively, these scores form what I call the retirement grade point average (GPA) matrix. And while opinions may vary on the specific scores, hopefully the overall ranking is intuitive.

Focusing first on the left side of the chart and retirement risk management attributes, you start by evaluating the lifetime payout income annuity (LPIA). As mentioned, the strength of this product lies in its promise to pay out a steady, fixed payment for as long as the policyholder lives. Because the retiree cannot outlive the guaranteed income that the LPIA provides, longevity risk is directly addressed and hedged. The product can even be viewed as a close substitute for the disappearing traditional pension. Accordingly, I assign the highest score of 5 to the LPIA for the longevity risk attribute.

Conversely, the LPIA scores the lowest on its ability to tackle inflation. In its basic form, a LPIA provides fixed payments in nominal terms. So the most common manifestation of the product does not avoid the erosion of purchasing power effect. Finally, I assign a somewhat neutral score to the LPIA for its ability to hedge against the sequence of returns risk. While the product does not explicitly provide insurance against an early bear market, it indirectly overcomes the risk, because payments are fixed and guaranteed regardless of market fluctuations.

What is Your Retirement Product GPA?

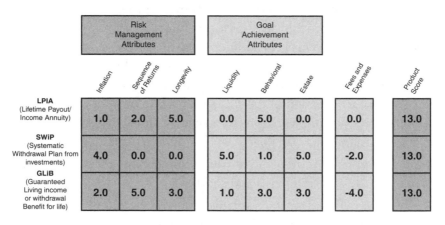

	Risk Management Attributes			Goal Achievement Attributes				
	Inflation	Sequence of Returns	Longevity	Liquidity	Behavioral	Estate	Fees and Expenses	Product Score
LPIA (Lifetime Payout/ Income Annuity)	1.0	2.0	5.0	0.0	5.0	0.0	0.0	13.0
SWiP (Systematic Withdrawal Plan from investments)	4.0	0.0	0.0	5.0	1.0	5.0	-2.0	13.0
GLiB (Guaranteed Living income or withdrawal Benefit for life)	2.0	5.0	3.0	1.0	3.0	3.0	-4.0	13.0

Figure 10.1   The different strategies, each with a grade point average.

Source: Moshe Milevsky and the IFID Centre, 2008.

Moving on to the SWiP category, Figure 10.1 shows a reversal in risk management strengths, compared to the LPIA: The product receives the highest grade for the inflation hedging attribute. The investment choices within a SWiP account are virtually endless and the underlying asset allocation is under the control of the investor. This allows him to select investments that tend to outpace the rate of inflation.

The SWiP ranks the lowest, however, for the sequence of returns attribute. It offers no protection against potential market drops in the fragile risk zone. This shortfall might result in a damaging and lasting financial effect on retirement. And while a SWiP allocation heavily weighted in fixed-income investments might overcome market volatility, it might lead to low growth. As a result, investments might not keep up with the rate of inflation and the retiree may "outlive" her funds.

Next, for its effectiveness as a longevity hedging tool, the SWiP account receives a score of 0. There are again no associated guarantees, and the investor is solely responsible for monitoring and adjusting the spending and investment policy to make the account last for the duration of retirement.

As for the GLiB category, the grades are mixed. These products score the highest among the three for their capability to hedge a retirement against the sequence of returns risk. As I mentioned earlier, implicit guarantees and promises are the core of GLiBs. Many of them promise *at least* the return of the initial investment, despite the performance of the market in the fragile risk zone. GLiBs are analogous to (albeit complex) long-term equity put options that can be purchased in the open market to provide downside protection on a portfolio. Thus, their embedded guarantees earn GLiBs the highest score for this attribute.

However, as I already mentioned, not all GLiBs are created equal. Only some variations offer a true form of longevity insurance that guarantees an income for life. As a result, the GLiBs fall short of the LPIA's high score on the longevity risk management attribute.

Finally, just as they vary in their ability to address longevity insurance, some GLiBs are superior to others in their effectiveness at hedging inflation. Although GLiBs do not typically provide explicit inflation protection, many offer systematic payment step-ups or increases that could potentially offset the impact of inflation. Hence, this product ranks between the SWiP and the LPIA for this attribute.

As you can see in Figure 10.1, the risk management attributes of the three retirement income products are only half of the story. The allocation among the products must be selected in the context of at least three goals: liquidity, behavioral "self-discipline," and estate.

For example, a total allocation to a LPIA would be inappropriate if the retiree's future goal was to leave a large sum to his estate. Likewise, the product's inherent design would not allow for a fluctuating spending rate or large lump sum withdrawals for unexpected cash needs. After all, the reason LPIAs are able to offer such effective longevity insurance is the complete irreversibility of the initial lump sum payment. Thus, for the LPIA's ability to address liquidity and estate goals, the product receives a score of 0.

On the other hand we assign a high score of 5 for the LPIA's capability to overcome potential behavioral mistakes that investors are prone to making. That is, many of us are susceptible to making irrational decisions and errors with our investments in the absence of restrictions or a guiding system in place. This can decrease the chances of meeting our spending goals in retirement. When the initial irreversible payment is made to the insurance company issuing the LPIA, the control over the investment management decisions is also transferred away from the investor. This leaves virtually no room for behavioral biases and blunders.

The SWiP once again earns the reversed ranking on this set of goal-achievement attributes. With a SWiP, the investor can meet liquidity needs and estate goals with the greatest ease because she retains control over asset allocation and withdrawal rate. But it is this exact same reason that leads to a score of only 1 for the SWiP's low effectiveness in helping the investor to avert behavioral mistakes.

Finally, only the GLiB's evaluation on goal-achievement attributes remains. First, the liquidity of an account with a GLiB benefit is somewhat restricted because of withdrawal limits imposed by the rider. Moreover, variable annuities restrict withdrawals beyond a certain limit by charging surrender fees. However, the policyholder does have a certain level of flexibility, even if it may come at a price. Thus the GLiB surpasses the SPIA with a score of 1 on this trait.

A GLiB rider can also be effective in addressing behavioral weaknesses, hence its score of 3. When purchasing a GLiB, the investor effectively purchases peace of mind, knowing he is protected in the fragile risk zone against poor market performance. As a result the investor needs not make any (possibly detrimental) moves to try and adjust his retirement investment and spending strategy.

Interestingly, the GLiB's estate goal achievement attribute is somewhat interconnected with the behavioral attribute. Analysis of extensive industry data suggests that because the investor is protected against a market downturn during sensitive years, she is more likely to opt for a riskier asset allocation within the variable annuity. This allocation could potentially result in higher growth over the long term that could be bequeathed at death. Of course, in some cases the variable annuity account may eventually be annuitized or irreversibly converted into a retirement income stream. When this takes place—just as in the case of the LPIA—no death benefit will be paid. This limitation on the estate goal within the GLiB category leads to a score of 3 for this product category.

The final step in the retirement product GPA matrix is the assignment of a relative score to the products based on the fees they charge and the computation of the final product score. The basic LPIA tends to be the cheapest product option from the perspective of fees and commissions. The GLiB is the highest because of the associated ongoing insurance fee that must be charged for the embedded guarantees. The account owner maintains some control over the fees charged by a SWiP because these vary with the selection of the underlying investments. As a result, its fees and expenses score falls between that of the other two income products.

With scores assigned to each product for each attribute in Figure 10.1, I can proceed with the simple addition of the seven numbers to arrive at an overall product score in the right column. No, it is not a coincidence that the three values are identical. The point here is that the three products are economically equal. Each offers a valuable benefit that is "paid for" via a trade-off in another risk management or goal achievement attribute. That is, one product might hedge against longevity risk but at the expense of an estate or a liquidity goal; another product might offer peace of mind through guarantees but at the price of higher product fees, and so on.

Figure 10.2 graphically illustrates the retirement income problem. How do you split your nest egg across the range of available products? On the one hand, a systematic withdrawal plan (SWiP) provides much liquidity and flexibility but is not necessarily sustainable. In contrast, the immediate annuity or lifetime payout annuity (LPiA) provides 100% sustainability but at the expense of liquidity, bequest, and flexibility. Finally, the variable annuity with the new generation of guaranteed living income benefit (GLiB) provides greater flexibility and sustainability, but is obviously more expensive and has higher fees compared to the other two product classes. So, how do you determine the optimal mix?

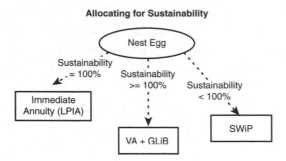

Figure 10.2   Split the nest egg three ways: You decide how.

Source: Moshe Milevsky and the IFID Centre, 2008.

The PrARI® methodology guides individuals in determining the suitable mix for their nest egg. To properly implement PrARI, we need a number of input variables. Retirement age, estimated retirement wealth, desired spending rate, as well as existing pension and social security income are just some of the variables that must be assessed as part of the planning process. Combined, these elements will induce a particular retirement sustainability quotient (RSQ)—this is the probability that the spending strategy will be sustainable and will not result in a spending shortfall. As well, the input variables will induce a corresponding expected discounted bequest (EDB)—the present value of the amount expected to be left to the estate. Moreover, varying the product allocations will change the value of the RSQ (captured by the horizontal X-axis) and EDB (captured by the vertical Y-axis), which then traces out a frontier displayed in Figure 10.3.

Finally, your retirement priorities would be assessed to select your optimal retirement product allocation along the frontier. When trying to pinpoint an appropriate product allocation, a guiding concept should be the economic trade-off that is implicit within any selected product allocation: namely, security for oneself versus security for one's heirs.

Figure 10.4 illustrates this trade-off in retirement for four selected spending rates from 4.8% to 5.8%. Each point along the four lines corresponds to a unique product allocation for a 62-year-old. Note that the precise optimal product allocations were determined using a proprietary algorithm called Optimal Product Allocation for Retirement Income (PrARI) developed by the QWeMA Group Inc.

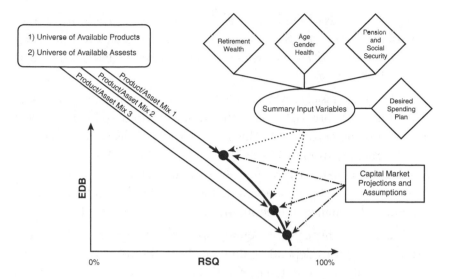

Figure 10.3   The retirement income frontier.

Source: Moshe Milevsky and the IFID Centre, 2008.

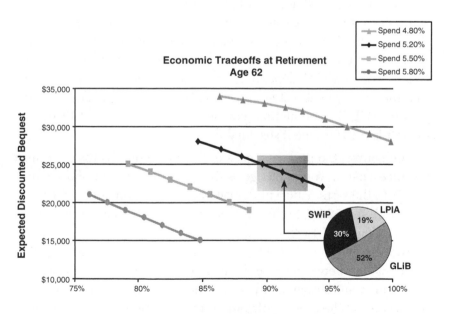

Figure 10.4   What is Harry's risk versus return?

Source: Moshe Milevsky and the IFID Centre, 2008.

On the X axis of the figure are the values of the Retirement Sustainability Quotient (RSQ). Notice that only strategies with an RSQ value of at least 75% are considered to be tolerable and are included in the chart.

Of course, it is clearly desirable to be on the right side of this spectrum; but this is precisely where the trade-off captured by the vertical Y axis must be considered. This is the expected discounted bequest (EDB), ranging from $10 to $35 per initial nest egg of $100. For each plotted line, a higher EDB value always comes at the "price" of a lower RSQ. That is, the bigger amount that is desired to be left to the estate, the lower the chance of meeting the annual spending goal.

Table 10.1 displays the actual "optimal" allocations to the three product categories depending on your desired level of retirement income security (represented by the RSQ value) versus your desire and interest to leave a legacy for your loved ones. For example, assume that you have $100,000 in your retirement nest egg, and that you desire to spend $5,200 adjusted for inflation on an annual basis. This translates into a real spending rate of 5.2%, which is reasonable although it certainly is not guaranteed to be sustainable. By reasonable I mean that the retirement sustainability quotient is somewhere between 95% and 85% depending on your product allocation. Notice that the more you allocate to products that contain guaranteed living benefits (GLiBs) and lifetime pay-out income annuities (LPIAs), the greater is the retirement sustainability quotient.

Of course, the price of a greater "sustainability" is that you must sacrifice a part of your estate goals. Notice that when you allocate only 18.9% to the systematic withdrawal plan and the remaining 29.1% to the LPIA and 52.0% to the variable annuity with a guaranteed living income benefit (GLiB), then although your RSQ value is 94.5%, the EDB value is a mere $22,000 of your original $100,000 nest egg. This is the tradeoff between risk and return in retirement. You can increase the security and sustainability of your desired retirement income, but it will come at the expense of your heirs and beneficiaries. If you want to leave as much as possible to the next generation, then obviously stay away from (expensive, irreversible) annuity products. On the other hand, if you primarily want to maximize sustainability and would like to bequeath the remaining funds, then your allocation to annuity instruments should be greater.

TABLE 10.1   Product Allocation: A More Technical Look
(Spend 5.2% of the Nest Egg, Adjusted for Inflation)

Lifetime Pay-out Income Annuities (LPIA)	Guarantee Living Income Benefits (GLiB)	Systematic Withdrawal Plan (SWiP)	Retirement Sustainability Quotient (RSQ)	Expected Discounted Bequest (EDB)
29.1%	52.0%	18.9%	94.45%	$22,000
23.9%	51.8%	24.3%	92.84%	$23,000
18.6%	51.6%	29.8%	91.23%	$24,000
13.3%	51.4%	35.3%	89.63%	$25,000
8.1%	51.2%	40.8%	88.02%	$26,000
2.8%	51.0%	46.2%	86.41%	$27,000
0.0%	37.2%	62.9%	84.63%	$28,000

Assumptions: Risk free rate = 3%; 100% equity allocation;

Equity: expected returns = 7%, volatility = 18%; GLiB insurance fee = 1.3%, LPIA insurance load = 7% of fair premium

Source: Moshe Milevsky and the IFID Centre, 2008.

Some Case Studies

Meet three hypothetical individuals named Albert, Denise, and Edward, all of whom are seeking retirement product allocation advice. Let's briefly examine their retirement priorities and economic trade-offs.

Albert's Top Retirement Priority: Large Bequest

Albert is 62-years-old and has spent most of his life working for the same company. He is thinking of taking early retirement, because as a result of his many years of service, he is entitled to a generous defined benefit (DB) pension that will provide him with approximately $45,000 per year, plus an annual cost-of-living adjustment. Moreover, in addition to his pension, he also has accumulated approximately $200,000 in a company 401(k) account that he plans to roll over into an IRA as soon as he retires. And so, Albert needs *product allocation* advice for his IRA. With the help of a professional financial advisor, Albert estimates that to properly finance the lifestyle he desires in retirement, he requires an additional inflation-adjusted income of approximately $9,600 per year; this is in addition to his $45,000 pension. In the language of retirement income planning, this translates into an inflation-adjusted withdrawal rate of 4.8% of his nest egg. Thus, given Albert's desired withdrawal rate of 4.8%, he faces an economic trade-off, which is represented by the top curve in Figure 10.4.

His choices are as follows. On the one hand, he can select a product allocation that will generate a nearly 100% probability of sustainability. This is the point on the line furthest along the horizontal RSQ axis. However notice that this point also corresponds to the lowest expected discounted bequest value of $28 per initial $100 (or $56,000 of his $200,000 nest egg). On the other hand, he can select the strategy that maximizes his EDB on the line, allowing him to leave an EDB of $34 per initial $100 (or $68,000 of his $200,000 nest egg) to his estate. However, this would require a sacrifice in the sustainability quotient. Notice that this is the point that has the lowest probability of success on the curve: 86%. Albert's true economic trade-off at retirement is between securing his income with the highest possible chance of success or taking some risk that he might have to reduce his standard of living in the future. The so-called payoff from the risk he takes is that his estate goals and bequest motives are achieved.

The choice of where to "sit" on the frontier traced out in Figure 10.4 is entirely up to Albert. In the end, given the heavy weighting on his estate goal, Albert decides to position himself on the point at which the estate goal is maximized and the sustainability is minimized. Once again, this is his choice. In the world of product allocation, this translates into the following allocation. The 88% bulk of his IRA is invested in a mutual fund or managed account and the desired income is generated using a systematic withdrawal plan (SWiP). The balance of 12% (that is, $24,000) is used to purchase a variable annuity with a GLiB rider. This particular strategy will allow him to leave an expected discounted bequest of $68,000 in present value terms. The probability of meeting his spending goal of $9,600 per year, that is, his RSQ, is approximately 86%. Likewise, no amount is allotted to the LPIA category. Recall from the PGA matrix that the product received a score of

0 on the estate attribute and, therefore, would not be well-suited for addressing Albert's main goal. In sum, given Albert's relatively low desired spending rate and desire to bequeath a large portion of his IRA to his children, he is counseled to adopt a product allocation of 88% SWiP, 12% GLiB, and 0% LPiA.

Denise's Top Retirement Priorities: Bequest and Sustainable Income

Denise is about to turn 62 years of age and retire. She has been looking forward to this stage of her life, much of which she plans to spend traveling the world with her husband. She has been employed in the public sector throughout most of her working years and will receive a reasonable inflation adjusted defined benefit pension as a result. In addition, being a diligent saver, she has accumulated a nest egg of $1 million and would like to withdraw an inflation-adjusted income of $55,000 or 5.5% of her nest egg to help finance the couple's retirement plans. Finally, Denise would like to leave a portion of her nest egg to her heirs as a bequest.

The trade-off that Denise faces is represented in the Figure 10.4 by the second line. She is presented with a choice of several strategies that would result in an expected discounted bequest ranging from $19 per initial $100 (or $190,000) to $25 per initial $100 (or $250,000). The corresponding retirement sustainability quotient ranges from 89% to 79%.

Denise feels that both goals—achieving a steady and sustainable spending rate of $55,000 per year, as well as leaving a bequest—are equally important. She feels that she can risk falling somewhat short of her target income because the couple can also rely on her pension and the husband's retirement income to meet their spending needs. As a result, she decides to compromise between her two goals and selects the following allocation strategy. The largest proportion (57%) is to be allocated to a SWiP account to address Denise's liquidity and estate goals, while the lesser allocations to the LPIA (12%) and GLiB (31%) categories will help address longevity and sequence of returns risk to achieve a reasonable retirement sustainability quotient.

Edward's Top Retirement Priority: High Retirement Income

Edward is 61-years-old and has been self-employed throughout his working years. He is only one year away from retirement and estimates that he will have accumulated $1.5 million in retirement savings. In planning his product allocation strategy for retirement, he identifies his main goal to be achieving a spending of $87,000 per year, after inflation. Edward is in excellent health; it should be noted that his parents lived well into their nineties.

As in the previous cases, the trade-off presented to Edward is illustrated in Figure 10.4 by the left line. In contrast to the other retirees, Edward is not concerned with leaving a significant sum to his estate. He hopes to perhaps leave only a portion of his nest egg to his favored charity and to cover any remaining expenses. Because Edward does not have a pension that will last for the remainder of his life, and given the good health experienced by him and his family, he is most concerned with maintaining a substantial spending rate and hedging against longevity risk.

Bearing in mind his financial circumstances and retirement priorities, Edward chooses the following product allocation: 32% will be allocated to the LPIA, 11% to the GLiB, and 58% to the SWiP. He will spend $87,000 per year in real dollars and achieve an expected discounted bequest value of $225,000 (or $15 per initial $100), which he finds to be adequate. The RSQ, or probability of meeting his spending goal is approximately 85%. Note that the 32% allocation to the LPIA category exceeds that of previous cases. This, of course, can be attributed to the product's excellent ability to hedge against longevity risk. The justification for the large allocation to the SWiP is the high associated liquidity that is needed for a high withdrawal rate. In sum, Edward will forego a large bequest goal for a high withdrawal rate with a maximized retirement sustainability quotient.

The Main Takeaway

The hypothetical case studies I have just illustrated obviously should not be taken literally as actual investment or insurance recommendations for real people. Rather, the aforementioned mini-stories should be viewed as tools for thinking about the characteristics that affect the economic tradeoffs in retirement. It is the beginning of a discussion rather than the end of a process.

Thus, for example, one glaring omission from all these simple stories is the precise role of life insurance in maximizing the estate value. After all, if the retiree is sufficiently well off so that he is never likely to exhaust his nest egg regardless of his spending rate, then life insurance is likely to be part of the optimal portfolio, at the very least for estate planning purposes. Likewise, the exact role of personal debt in the form of reverse mortgages or home equity loans—even at the advanced stage of the lifecycle—is yet another dimension to a healthy product allocation diet. Another product that certainly belongs in the optimal retirement portfolio is long-term care insurance, which is yet another part of a prudent risk management strategy.

Guarantees Make People Feel More Comfortable

Up until now I have discussed the rather theoretical models and processes for how people *should* be making decisions about their retirement products, pension annuities, and insurance riders. However, it's always interesting to see what investors and soon-to-be retirees are doing in practice, and so I conclude this chapter with a brief discussion of how people actually behave when it comes to their product and asset allocations.

Some convincing evidence emerges from a large database of variable annuity policyholders that the researchers at LIMRA International have been kind enough to allow us to probe and dissect (anonymously, of course). It turns out that when investors purchase guaranteed living benefits, the perception of these attained guarantees gives them the confidence to modify their investment behavior. Namely, they unequivocally accept greater equity market risk simply because they have this insurance; it remains to be seen how this will impact the market, availability, and pricing of these benefits in the long run.

Together with a graduate student of mine, we reviewed the overall asset allocation of variable annuity account holders and classified their investment asset allocations within these products into two

distinct categories: risky and risk-free. We were interested to see how
these allocations varied by age as well as the types of guarantees (riders) selected. The kinds of questions we were interested in were: Do
older policyholders allocate less wealth to riskier asset classes? Do
younger policyholders embrace riskier asset classes? How does this
change when various insurance riders and guarantees are elected?
Figure 10.5 provides a graphical illustration of the main results for just
one of the insurance companies we analyzed.

Do Guarantees Lead to Riskier Allocations?

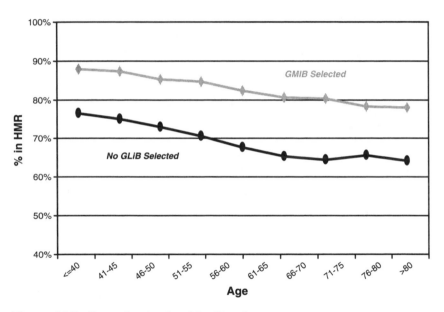

Figure 10.5   I'm going to shoot for the stars.

Source: Moshe Milevsky and the IFID Centre, 2008.

The X axis displays the age of the policyholder when she opened
or purchased the variable annuity. Our data goes from under age 40
on the left side, up to age 80 and beyond on the right side. On the Y
axis we plotted the average amount that was allocated to the High and
Medium Risk (HMR) categories, which included equity-based funds
as well as real estate and international investments.

As you can see, the older investors tend to allocate a smaller
amount to risky subaccounts within their variable annuities. This is

fairly consistent with intuition and what economists call life cycle theory of investing.

Another finding is that when no guaranteed living benefit (GLiB)—that is, extra levels of protection—was selected by the client, the level of risky equity exposure within the account tended to be lower, by about 10 to 30 percentage points, compared to the basic case. We think this is the more interesting result.

In other words, roughly half of the more than 100,000 policies purchased contained no living benefits. In those cases the amount of equity exposure tended to be much lower compared to the policies in which the riders were elected (and paid for).

Is this terribly surprising? Not really. Most advisors will readily agree that these guaranteed living benefits provide some comfort and help investors accept more risk. These numbers support this fact and provide some estimates on the magnitude of this effect.

Note that this pattern—a GLiB selected is associated with greater risk exposure—is consistent across all insurance companies we analyzed. This is not just a fluke associated with one or two companies, or a given living benefit rider, or a particular company's asset allocation restrictions.

Remember that individuals with more aggressive equity allocations essentially have a higher exposure to the stock market compared to fixed-income products, which in the long run is the winning asset class. In fact, the extra investment return that one obtains might offset the higher fees that are required to pay for this protection. Or here is a slightly offbeat way to think about this: A GLiB is a therapist that pays for itself!

Of course, psychology aside, one has to wonder: Is this extra level of risk justified in theory? For this, I believe the answer is a definite, "yes." After all, if you are granted an "equity put option," (recall that this is a type of insurance on your portfolio) how else would you behave? Stated differently, why bother protecting or insuring a portfolio (that is, asset mix) that has little chance of requiring protection in the long run? If you want to hold bonds and other fixed income products in your portfolio, don't waste valuable protection/insurance dollars and find some other silo in your personal balance to hold those low-risk instruments.

Now, along the same lines, some commentators have argued that a variable annuity with a GLiB can actually be treated as a "bond substitute" in the overall asset allocation. They go so far as to view the entire V.A. + GLiB package as a bond. This, I tend to disagree with. Remember that you cannot cash in and get your money back at anytime without incurring withdrawal fees, and you must wait (for a long time) to get all your money back. Thus, in some cases you have to wait for decades before you get the guaranteed return that is promoted on these products. This is very different from a conventional bond.

That said, once again, granting investors an equity put option should give the investor greater confidence to take on equity market risk, and one doesn't require a bond classification to achieve this result. It is a different product class. It is not a bond, stock, or balanced fund—it is a new category.

The Bottom Line

Notwithstanding the disparate threads I weaved into this chapter, the main practical takeaway point is as follows: My extensive analysis, and the view of many of my esteemed colleagues in academia and beyond, leads me to conclude that in most cases retirees will *not* be able to finance a sustainable retirement income with only one or two traditional product classes, basic mutual funds, or conventional income annuities. Indeed, all three product categories—income annuities, mutual funds, and variable annuities with embedded guarantees—mixed and matched in various combinations are required to maximize one's retirement sustainability quotient (RSQ). As you get closer to retirement, you will develop a better sense of your needs and feasible estate goals. We leave it in the hands of individuals and their financial advisors to determine the exact proportions that balance their own retirement risks with the desire for a financial legacy. In sum, retirement income is not an all-or-nothing, now-or-never proposition. Diversify across products and across time.

Summary

- At retirement one should strive to create a diversified portfolio of products that protect against various retirement risks. Take a portion of your 401(k), 403(b), IRA, or any other retirement plan, tax sheltered or not, and make sure to allocate a portion of the money to some sort of annuity instrument, whether fixed or variable, immediate or deferred—get some mortality credits.

- In the accumulation phase, asset allocation is the most important decision that people face with their investments. If you allocate too much of your retirement nest egg to any one asset class, economic sector, or industry, you are setting yourself up for disappointment. Diversify your assets. In the retirement income phase, however, product allocation will become (even) more important.

- PrARI methodology is one example of how individuals and their advisors determine and decide how to split or distribute their retirement nest egg across the wide universe of choices. This process should not be ad hoc. Make sure there is a sound justification for your retirement product allocation.

Endnotes

[1] Note that PrARI® is a registered trademark owned by the QWeMA Group and used with its permission.

This chapter has been heavily influenced by extensive discussions I have had with financial advisors, insurance practitioners, and many individual retirees over the last few years. I owe each of them a debt of gratitude for helping me refine my thinking on the importance of product allocation in retirement. The cases I have used in this chapter draw heavily from a white paper that I wrote for MetLife Investors in mid-2008, and I would like to thank them for permission to reproduce a few of the charts and examples. A much more detailed statistical analysis and discussion of the asset allocation within variable annuities is available in Milevsky and Kyrychenko (2008). The article by Ameriks, Veres, and Warshawsky (2001) was one of the first to make the argument that a retirement income portfolio should contain some mixture of basic income annuities to increase sustainability. The role and importance of annuities in a retirement income portfolio is discussed at length in the book by Brown,

Mitchell, Poterba, and Warshawsky (2001). The paper by Chen and Milevsky (2003) forms the basis of a patented product allocation model that assists individuals in allocating wealth between immediate annuities and traditional investments using the economic concept of utility. As in previous chapters, I have shied away from giving references and citations to academic papers that are too theoretical or highly mathematical, but simply advise the reader to consult the Milevsky (2006) book for a more extensive list of technical references. The final examples and case studies in this chapter utilizing three different retirement income products including GLiBs, as well as measuring their impact on RSQ/EDB, were generated by the QWeMA Group's PrARI methodology.

11

Conclusion: Plan for Managing Your Retirement Risk

Professor Richard Thaler from the University of Chicago and Professor Shlomo Benartzi from UCLA have devoted a substantial part of their careers to studying the financial mistakes and monetary blunders that people make in their daily lives. Apparently even smart people are not immune. These two researchers are leaders in the nascent field of behavioral finance, which argues that consumers are not cold, calculating machines that optimize their decisions in a rigorous mathematical fashion, but instead they adopt simple general rules for financial decision making, which often leads them far astray.

One of the most egregious behavioral "sins" these two researchers have identified is the tendency of too many Americans to allocate too much of their 401(k) plan—and even their own investments—to company stock. Apparently, more than five million Americans have over 60% of their retirement savings invested in their own company stock. Note that this is well after the notorious cases of Enron or WorldCom, where employees discovered the ruinous risks of such a myopic strategy. Even more surprising, ongoing surveys and focus groups conducted with these same employees indicate that they simply do not view this behavior as problematic. They think it is normal and healthy to invest in "things they know" because they can keep an eye on their investments. This optimism stands in contrast to the fact there is absolutely no evidence that employees have any superior ability to outguess the market or the experts regarding the performance of the stocks they hold and the companies they work for.

One of the main arguments in this book is that many of these five million Americans who are engaging in this risky practice might be dead wrong. They are improperly investing their human capital and financial capital in the same economic basket, and their retirement might be at risk. Indeed, the evidence suggests that we have a long way to go before individuals truly consider the risk and return characteristics of their human capital and invest their financial capital in a way that balances their comprehensive risks. Hopefully, this book will help along this path. Remember, your 401(k) is a number, not a pension. It is up to you to manage and grow your nest egg so that it can eventually be converted and allocated into a pension.

And so, in this concluding chapter, I try to bring the previous chapters together by reviewing the main highlights and then explaining how to formulate a proper retirement plan given all the tools we have acquired along the way.

Retirement Income Planning Is the Goal

At the university where I am a faculty member, I teach a popular 12-week course on personal financial planning to third- and fourth-year undergraduate students. During the semester, I try to cover the entire life cycle of financial issues, from cradle to grave. In the first few weeks, I spend quite a bit of class time on basic topics such as financial budgeting, managing credit card debt, coping with student loans, and so on. I usually get full attendance and engaged interest during these early lectures. In fact, sometimes I get even more than full attendance from nonregistered, yet interested students, who want to learn whether leasing is in fact better than buying a car, or whether ETFs are better or worse than index funds for the cost-conscious do-it-yourself investor. They are surprised when I preach that debt can be good, as I explained in Chapter 4, "Debt Can Be Good at All Ages." They absolutely resonate with my message that human capital is valuable and should be treated as an asset class to be hedged and insured. In fact, even the topic of life insurance, which I mentioned back in Chapter 2, "Insurance Is a Hedge for Human Capital," appears interesting to them, perhaps due to some morbid curiosity.

Then, somewhere toward the latter part of the semester, as things are winding down around week number eight or nine, I get to the topic of pensions and retirement income planning. Here I tell them about the pension annuities I introduced in Chapter 9, "Annuities Are Personal Pensions," as well as some of the demographic trends in aging. And, as much as it pains me to admit this, the attendance isn't great for that lecture. I'm lucky if I get 60% of my enrolled students, and many of those who do bother to show up spend much of the time text-messaging, pod-casting, and whatever else they can do to pass the time. The following week, which is devoted to estate planning, is even worse. In fact—and I'm only half joking here—if you have some extra altruistic energy on your hands and want to take on a challenge, try spending time with a bunch of teenagers explaining the minutia of calculating Social Security payments early on a Monday morning, no less.

And to be honest, I can't say I blame them. These kids are just not interested in retirement income planning. It is 40 years ahead of its time for them. To many of them that might as well be infinity. They are concerned with finding their dream job, getting rid of their student loan debt, and hopefully accumulating some savings. Even the topic of buying a home is distant to them. The pension is outside their realm of experience.

Yet, when I have the occasional chance to interact with students' parents and grandparents, the situation is very different. When I mention that I also teach and do research on pensions and retirement income planning, I feel like the only doctor at an evening cocktail party. Everyone wants free advice.

In fact, the personal interest in pension matters extends to my academic colleagues at the University. Around the age of retirement, all members of our pension plan must decide whether to take a lump-sum settlement and invest and manage it themselves, or whether to keep the money in the plan and instead receive a monthly income. Many of these professors have heard that I might "know something" about this issue, and I get a steady stream of biology, chemistry, and engineering professors visiting my office for a consultation around the time of their big decision. They are wondering whether they should take the money and run, hoping to get a better income themselves. (Interestingly, I don't get many humanities professors. I'm not sure why.)

But yet, the topic of pensions is more than just a matter of demographic interest. When I pose the question to my undergraduate students—which retirement arrangement would you rather have, defined benefit (DB) or defined contribution (DC)?—most of them select the DC plan. Some of them justify their decision with some fairly persuasive arguments. They point out that they will likely be working for a number of different employers over the course of their life. Some of them will be spending time in different countries, or at least industries. Few, if any, believe (or even dream) they will be working for one company over the course of 30 years. They, therefore, need retirement savings with mobility and flexibility. Alas, a defined benefit plan with its rigid formulas based on years of service and final salary would make little sense to them. It is a relic from an industrial past. Indeed, this is likely why so many employees are content with 401(k) and IRA plans. The employer's only responsibility is to contribute 5% to 10% of their annual salary cost to this piggy bank, and the employee is responsible for everything else. Employees take the risk and get the reward.

The statistics I presented in the Introduction confirms this way of thinking. Many of the companies freezing or converting their defined benefit (DB) pensions and replacing them with defined contribution (DC) plans are doing so *partly as a result of the demand from employees.*

And yet, as the trends in aging, which I discussed in Chapter 7, "Longevity Is a Blessing and a Risk," continue to develop over time, the topic of pension and retirement income will only grow in importance. Remember that retirees face a number of unique financial risks that are not (as) relevant earlier on in life. As I explained in Chapter 7, retirees face longevity risk, which is the uncertainty of their life horizon and its costs. Retirees face unique inflation risk, based on the data I presented in Chapter 5, "Personal Inflation and the Retirement Cost of Living." Finally, they have to deal with a particular type of financial market risk, which has been dubbed the term *sequence of returns.* So, the risks are new and different, and you will need a different strategy.

As you can see from Table 11.1, approximately 80% of the income being received by individuals above the age of 85 is longevity-insured. The remaining 20% of their monthly income might be exhausted prior to the end of their life. For younger individuals the percent that is longevity insured is even lower.

TABLE 11.1   **What Fraction of Elderly Income Contains Longevity Insurance That Can't Be Outlived? (Average for U.S. Population)**

Age Group	Income in 2004
65–69	49.9%
70–74	62.4%
75–79	70.4%
80–84	75.1%
85+	80.1%

Social Security, Pensions, and Annuities

Source: Employee Benefit Research Institute, 2006.

Step 1: Get a Retirement Needs Analysis

Obviously, boiling down the entire topic of retirement income planning into a 30-second sound bite is impossible. This is likely one of most complicated calculations that an individual must make over the course of his life, and even the great Allan Greenspan has been quoted as saying this! That said, I can provide some general rules on how to think about this problem.

So, when *you* are ready to seriously think about the financing of your retirement, the first step is to sit down (perhaps with a financial advisor) and carefully estimate what you will need in retirement. I mentioned this process in Chapter 8, "Spending Your Retirement in Monte Carlo," and will briefly review the main ideas here again. Some people dismiss the importance of a formal written *retirement needs analysis* altogether. Or some confuse it with its close cousin—the *retirement wants analysis*, which is much more than your needs. Either way the exercise is informative. Add up the estimated annual cost of all the things you simply can't live without. These can be items as basic as rent, electricity, and heating, all the way up to the annual cost of a golf club membership, or lease payment on the Mercedes Benz. Do your best to come up with a rough annual retirement needs estimate. Remember, though, it is a number that will not stand still. It is a moving target over time. This is because you will likely experience a higher and unique inflation during retirement. Either way, don't move to the next step until you have this needs estimate. Also, remember these are your needs, not your wants.

Step 2: Determine Your Income Gap

The next step is to add up the sources of all of your retirement income benefits or guaranteed pension benefits. Start by getting your Social Security estimate and move on to any DB pensions you are entitled to from work. Make sure to differentiate income sources that are adjusted annually for inflation, such as Social Security and many state pension plans, from income sources that are not adjusted for inflation.

The difference between your retirement needs and your guaranteed retirement income is your *income gap*. This number can be $10,000 or $100,000 or $1,000,000 but is truly the most important number in retirement income planning.

For now, if 85% of your retirement income needs will be supplied by a Defined Benefit (DB) pension that generates inflation adjusted income, then you are hedged against most of your retirement risks. Stated differently, if your income gap is a mere 15% of your projected income needs, then you do not need to get any insurance or other forms of guarantees and protection. For many people though, an 85% replacement rate from pensions and Social Security, is not very likely. Refer back to Figure 8.1 for a graphical illustration of this calculation.

Now, let's move to the asset side of your personal balance sheet and the investment assets that are available to close the income gap. Presumably, as I explained in Chapter 1, "You, Inc.," you have by now converted most of your human capital into financial capital, which is your financial nest egg. Add up the value of the 401(k), 403(b), IRA, stocks, bonds, mutual funds, and other investment-based (that is, DC) pensions. Anything you can and are willing to sell should be included in this calculation of wealth. At this point you should not include the value of your house unless you plan to sell, move out, and use the funds to generate your retirement income. For now, this is your "financial assets number."

We are now ready for the big question. What is the mathematical ratio between the market value of your financial assets and your income gap? The larger the mathematical ratio is, the better your situation. For example, if your financial asset value is $1,000,000 and your income gap is $50,000, then your ratio is 20. But, if you have the same $1,000,000 in financial assets and your income gap is a higher $100,000 then your ratio is 10.

You will notice that so far I have not mentioned anything about your age, your gender, your marital status, or even your health. The calculation of the mathematical ratio between your wealth and your income gap doesn't depend on any of these demographic factors.

Now you are ready for some general recommendations. Please don't take this as investment advice, but rather as a blueprint for discussion.

TABLE 11.2   The Two Dimensions of Retirement Income Risk Management: How Much Wealth Do You Have to Finance Your Income Gap?

Retirement At Age 65	Income Gap <= 10%	Income Gap = +/– 25%	Income Gap = +/– 50%	Income Gap >= 80%
Wealth / Gap >=35	A+	A	B+	B
Wealth / Gap +/–25	B	C	C–	C–
Wealth / Gap +/–20	C	D	D–	D–
Wealth / Gap +/–15	D+	E	E	E
Wealth / Gap <= 10	E	F	F	F

Grade Legend:

A: You are in great shape. Don't worry about insuring any retirement risks. You can finance your income gap using a systematic withdrawal plan. However, make sure to invest your nest egg in a portfolio of diversified stocks and some inflation-adjusted bonds, and then periodically withdraw your income needs.

B: You are in good shape, although you might want to consider allocating a token 5% to 10% of your nest egg to protect against longevity risk, either using an immediate annuity or a variable annuity with a guaranteed living income benefit, especially if you are not willing to consider your personal residence as an eventual retirement income vehicle.

C: You should have enough, but you might consider allocating 10% to 20% to one of the many pension-like annuity instruments to help manage retirement risks, especially longevity risk. The exact amount would depend on the strength of your bequest motives, or how much of your financial estate you would like to leave to the next generation.

D: You are at the lower edge of income sustainability. This is where product allocation is most important and has the greatest impact. You should consider allocating 20% to 40% to annuity products with an emphasis on instruments that protect against longevity risk and the risk of sequence of returns.

E: It's going to be very tight. That said, you might want to consider allocating 10% to 20% of your wealth to some sort of annuity instrument with insurance against longevity risk and sequence of returns, especially if there is no flexibility in your spending. You might want to delay retirement for a few years.

F: Not good. At some point during your retirement, you will be forced to reduce your standard of living. You should consider delaying retirement for a few years. Don't try to gamble or speculate your way out of this problem.

As you can see from the table, for those retirees and near-retirees who have 90% of their income guaranteed from pensions plus Social

Security, they don't have to worry about product allocation or converting their nest egg into more pension income. Indeed, the billionaire Bill Gates does not need an annuity. He will never outlive his money, even if he doesn't have a defined benefit pension from Microsoft.

Obviously, many variations exist on Table 11.2. Needless to say, if you are thinking of retiring at a younger age (say 60 or 55), then your investment wealth multiple—the first column in Table 11.2—should be higher to get a high grade in the safe region. Likewise, if you are retiring in your early or late 70s, you might not need as much. Also, if you are trying to protect a spouse and are planning for two people, then you should do these calculations jointly. Compute your total income gap and the total amount of assets to support that gap. Also, and just as importantly, there are health risks that go beyond the financial realm, which is why you should consider long-term care insurance, or at the very least learn something about it, so that you can talk intelligently about why you are not insuring against this risk. This is the beginning of a planning process, not the end. A new generation of retirement income products are now available. Figure 11.1 is just one indication that there is more innovation to come.

Financial Times, June 12, 2004

Figure 11.1   Innovation in the insurance industry.

In sum, the money in your 401(k), 403(b), or IRA plan is just a random number. Hopefully it's a big number, but by now you should know that it's not a pension. That part is up to you. So, don't let your fickle moods, fears, and phobias exert undue influence on the composition of your nest egg. Rather, use the unique nature and composition of your human capital to approach the management of your financial capital. Think and manage risk comprehensively, like the chief financial officer of You, Inc. Your future depends on it!

Endnotes

Benartzi and Thaler (2007) review the many biases that impact retirement saving behavior. They have collectively and individually conducted and reported on many experiments in behavioral finance and are two of my favorite authors and pioneers in this field. Belsky and Gilovich (1999) and Bazerman (1999) authored two great and readable books on the systematic mistakes we make with money. Finally, Swenson (2005) and Malkiel (2003) are references for the individuals who truly want to embark on this journey themselves, with low costs, low fees—and no one to blame if something goes wrong.

Appendix_____

Additional References and Notes

For further information about retirement income planning, investing your human capital and some of the other ideas presented in this book, please visit The IFID Centre's website at www.ifid.ca or see some of the following references. Note that I have been careful to pick articles and books that are relatively accessible (that is, free of equations).

Aaron, Henry J., editor (1999), *Behavioral Dimensions of Retirement Economics*, Brookings Institution Press, Washington.

Ameriks, John, R. Veres and M. J. Warshawsky (2001), "Making Retirement Income Last a Lifetime," *Journal of Financial Planning*, December, Article 6 (www.journalfp.net).

Baldwin, Ben G. (1994), *The New Life Insurance Investment Advisor* (revised edition), McGraw-Hill, New York.

Bazerman, Max H. (1999), *Smart Money Decisions: Why You Do What You Do with Money (And How to Change for the Better)*, John Wiley and Sons, Inc.

Becker, Gary S. (1993), *Human Capital: A Theoretical and Empirical Analysis with Special Reference to Education*, 3rd edition, University of Chicago Press.

Belsky, Gary and Tom Gilovich (1999), *Why Smart People Make Big Money Mistakes and How to Correct Them: Lessons from the New Science of Behavioral Economics*, Simon & Schuster, New York.

Benartzi, Shlomo and Richard H. Thaler (2007), "Heuristics and Biases in Retirement Savings Behavior," *The Journal of Economic Perspectives*, Vol. 21(3): 81–104.

Bernstein, Peter L. (1992), *Capital Ideas: The Improbable Origins of Modern Wall Street*, The Free Press, New York.

Bengen, W. P. (2001), "Conserving Client Portfolios During Retirement," *Journal of Financial Planning*, May, Article 14, (www.journalfp.net).

Bodie, Zvi, Robert C. Merton, and William F. Samuelson (1992), "Labor Supply Flexibility and Portfolio Choice in a Life Cycle Model," *Journal of Economic Dynamics and Control*, Vol. 16(3): 327–449.

Bodie, Zvi and Michael J. Clowes (2003), *Worry-Free Investing : A Safe Approach to Achieving Your Lifetime Financial Goals*, Financial Times/Prentice Hall Books.

Brown, Jeff R., Olivia S. Mitchell, James M. Poterba, and Mark J. Warshawsky (2001), *The Role of Annuity Markets in Financing Retirement*, The MIT Press, Cambridge, Massachusetts.

Campbell, John Y. and Martin Feldstein, editors (2001), *Risk Aspects of Investment-Based Social Security Reform*, National Bureau of Economic Research, University of Chicago Press.

Campbell, John and Luis Viceira (2002), *Strategic Asset Allocation: Portfolio Choice for Long-term Investors*, Oxford University Press, UK.

Chen, Peng and Moshe A. Milevsky (2003), "Merging Asset Allocation and Longevity Insurance: An Optimal Perspective on Payout Annuities," *Journal of Financial Planning*, June, pp. 64–72.

Clark, Robert L., Richard V. Burkhauser, Marilyn Moon, Joseph F. Quinn, and Timothy M. Smeeding (2004), *The Economics of an Aging Society*, Blackwell Publishing, Malden, Massachusetts.

Eisenberg, Lee (2006), *The Number: A Completely Different Way to Think About the Rest of Your Life*, Simon & Schuster Adult Publishing Group, New York.

Evensky, Harold and Deena B. Katz, editors (2004), *The Investment Think Tank: Theory, Strategy and Practice for Advisors*, Bloomberg Press, Princeton.

Evensky, Harold and Deena B. Katz, editors (2006), *Retirement Income Redesigned: Master Plans for Distribution*, Bloomberg Press, Princeton.

Feinberg, Kenneth R. (2005), *What is Life Worth?: The Unprecedented Effort to Compensate the Victims of 9/11*, PublicAffairs.

Graham, Benjamin (2003), *The Intelligent Investor* (revised edition), with New Commentary by Jason Zweig, HarperCollins.

Goetzmann, William N. (1993), "The Single Family Home in the Investment Portfolio," *Journal of Real Estate Finance and Economics*, Vol. 6: 201–222.

Ho, Kwok, Moshe A. Milevsky, and Chris Robinson (1994), "How to Avoid Outliving Your Money," *Canadian Investment Review*, Vol. 7(3): 35–38.

Ibbotson, Roger, Moshe A. Milevsky, Peng Chen, and Kevin Zhu (2007), *Lifetime Financial Advice: Human Capital, Asset Allocation, and Insurance*, research monograph, CFA Institute, April 2007.

Jagannathan, Ravi and Narayan R. Kocherlakota (1996), "Why Should Older People Invest Less in Stocks Than Younger People?" *Federal Reserve Bank of Minneapolis Quarterly Review*, Summer 1996, Vol. 20(3): 11–23.

Kotlikoff, Laurence J. and Scott Burns (2004), *The Coming Generational Storm: What You Need to Know About America's Economic Future*, The MIT Press, Cambridge, USA.

Lee, Hye K. and Sherman Hanna (1995), "Investment Portfolios and Human Wealth," *Financial Counseling and Planning*, Vol. 6: 147–152.

Lleras, Miguel P. (2004), *Investing in Human Capital: A Capital Markets Approach to Student Funding*, Cambridge University Press, UK.

Lowenstein, Roger (2005), "We Regret to Inform You That You No Longer Have a Pension," *New York Times Magazine*, October 30, Section 6.

Malkiel, Burton G. (2003), *A Random Walk Down Wall Street: The Time Tested Strategy for Successful Investing*, W.W. Norton and Company, New York.

Markowitz, Harry M. (1991), "Individual Versus Institutional Investing," *Financial Services Review*, Vol. 1(1): 9–22.

Milevsky, Moshe A. and Aron A. Gottesman (2004), *Insurance Logic: Risk Management Strategies for Canadians*, 2nd Edition, Captus Press, Toronto.

Milevsky, Moshe A. and Thomas S. Salisbury (2006), "Financial Valuation of Guaranteed Minimum Withdrawal Benefits," *Insurance: Mathematics and Economics*, Vol. 38(1): 21–38.

Milevsky, Moshe A. and Steven Posner (2001), "The Titanic Option: Valuation of Guaranteed Minimum Death Benefits in Variable Annuities and Mutual Funds," *Journal of Risk and Insurance*, Vol. 68(1): 55–79.

Milevsky, Moshe A. and Vladyslav Kyrychenko (2008), "Portfolio Choice with Puts: Evidence from Variable Annuities," *Financial Analysts Journal*, May/June, volume.

Milevsky, Moshe A. and Keke Song (2008), "Do Markets Like Frozen DB Plans: An Event Study," working paper, The IFID Centre.

Milevsky, Moshe A. (2006), *The Calculus of Retirement Income: Financial Models for Pension Annuities and Life Insurance*, March 2006, Cambridge University Press.

Mitchell, Olivia and Kent Smetters, editors (2003), *The Pension Challenge: Risk Transfers and Retirement Income Security*, Oxford University Press, Oxford, UK.

Modigliani, Franco (1986), "Life Cycle, Individual Thrift and the Wealth of Nations," *The American Economic Review*, Vol. 76(3): 297–313.

Munnell, Alicia and Annika Sunden (2003), *Coming Up Short: The Challenge of 401(k) Plans*, Brookings Institution Press.

Olshansky, Jay and Bruce A. Carnes (2001), *The Quest for Immortality: Science at the Frontiers of Aging*, W.W. Norton & Company, New York.

Ostaszewski, K. (2003), "Is Life Insurance a Human Capital Derivatives Business?" *Journal of Insurance Issues*, Vol. 26(1): 1–14.

Reichenstein, William and Dovalee Dorsett (1995), *Time Diversification Revisited*, research monograph, CFA Institute, February 1995.

Salsbury, Gregory (2006), *But What if I Live? The American Retirement Crisis*, The National Underwriter Company, Cincinnati, Ohio.

Siegel, Jeremy J. (2002), *Stocks for the Long Run: The Definitive Guide to Financial Market Returns and Long-Term Investment Strategies* (3rd edition), McGraw-Hill, New York.

Swensen, David F. (2005), *Unconventional Success: A Fundamental Approach to Personal Investment*, Free Press, Simon & Schuster, New York.

Taleb, Nassim N. (2001), *Fooled By Randomness: The Hidden Role of Chance in the Markets and in Life*, Texere, New York.

INDEX

Numerics

401(a) plans, xix
401(k) plans, xix
   diversification, 38
   General Motors (GM), xvii
403(b) plans, xix
1992 Nobel Laureate in
   Economics, 16

A

Abaimova, Anna, 96
accounts
   diversification, xv
   self-directed, xix
adjustable rate mortgage (ARM), xv
advanced life delayed annuity
   (ALDA), 167
advantages of annuities, 149-152
allocation
   assets, 46-52
      sustainability, effects on,
      134, 138
   product
      case studies, 175-176, 179
      guarantees, 179-182
      inflation risk, 164-165
      longevity risk, 164
      overview of, 163-164
      sequence of returns, 165-175
American life expectancy, 164

analysis
   debt, 60
   needs
      conducting, 118, 120-129
      income gaps, determining,
      190-193
      risk management, 189
   portfolios, 68-72
   retirement
      income, 96-105
      risk, 129-134
   risk management, 185-187
annual percentage rate (APR), 90
annuities
   advantages of, 149-152
   fees, 157-159
   immediate, 154-156
   overview of, 141-148
   tontine, 152-154
   types of, 148-149
   variable (VA), 156
arithmetic average (AM), 131
assessment of net worth, 13
assets
   allocation, 46-52
      effect on sustainability,
      134, 138
   needs analysis, conducting, 118,
      120-129
   risk, formulas, 129-134
   worth, determining, 4-10, 13-18
automotive industry, retirement
   trends of, xxi

The Oldest Stage of Age

How old age comes and happens,
Shall I tell you? Here I go.
Your hair grows white and grey,
Oh so pretty shall I say.
A stick molds in your hand,
It's what I call a wooden cane.
Some cotton grows from your chin,
And your knees begin to shrink and shake,
Until a grandma dwarf begins to take your place.
First stage your teeth grow cavities,
And then they all come out,
Just wait until the doctor cries to make all of them false.
One day you are too short,
And you can not drive to work.
So your boss may come and tell you,
Get your pension stay at home.
Don't feel bad if this doesn't happen to you,
One day you will meet someone who it happened to.

Dahlia D. Milevsky
Age 10